QUESTIONS &ANSWERS

ABOUT BACKYARD BIRDS

The Minnesota Ornithologists' Union

Jim Williams and Anthony Hertzel

Adventure Publications, Inc.
Cambridge, MN

acknowledgments

We owe special thanks to Ingrid Sundstrom, editor of the Home and Garden section of the *Minneapolis Star Tribune* during the period when most of this material was written. In addition to being a good editor, she was gentle and fair. She always made our copy better. The same can be said for Connie Nelson, now editor of the section. Thanks to the Board of Directors of the MOU for its encouragement and enthusiasm for the project. Special thanks to Carrol Henderson of the Minnesota Department of Natural Resources. He reviewed the manuscript of this book, offering many helpful suggestions and improvements. Thanks also to Kim Eckert and Dave Benson who reviewed earlier drafts of this book. And thanks to Jude Hughes-Williams for her skillful review of drafts of our *Star Tribune* articles. She smoothed many edges.

Jim Williams and Anthony Hertzel

All proceeds from the sale of this book go directly to benefit the Minnesota Ornithologists' Union, a non-profit organization dedicated to the understanding of the birds of Minnesota.

Cover Photo by Adam Jones, Dembinsky Photo Associates

All other photos by Dudley Edmondson

Book design and illustrations by Jonathan Norberg

Table of Contents

Questions and Answers

Chapter Five: Sightings and Questions

Chapter Six: Birds Throughout the Year

introduction

Birdfeeding and birdwatching have rapidly grown in popularity in recent years. For some people, birds are a casual interest, for others a hobby, and for the most passionate an obsession. Whatever your level of interest, you are one of almost 60 million Americans who find wild birds fascinating.

The *Minneapolis Star Tribune* recognized this a few years ago and asked the Minnesota Ornithologists' Union (MOU) if it could provide information about backyard birds, about attracting them, feeding them and enjoying them. The MOU is Minnesota's largest bird club. Over 60 years old, it has more than 1,400 members. The MOU agreed to provide essays on backyard birding and to answer questions from readers.

What you see in this book comes from the past pages of the Home and Garden section of the *Minneapolis Star Tribune*. It is used here with the gracious permission of the newspaper.

The questions, their answers and the essays are pertinent to most areas of the Upper Midwest. If you have Black-capped Chickadees and American Goldfinches in your neighborhood, this book will be a good birding companion.

feeding

Who Eats What?

Birds, when choosing food, aren't nearly as fussy as some children I know, but they do have preferences. Choosing a particular food to feed your backyard birds gives you an element of control over which species come to visit. A wonderful chart, entitled "Who Likes What?" has been published by the Audubon Chapter of Minneapolis.

The chart lists all of the seed choices routinely found for sale in wild bird stores and other seed outlets, then indicates which birds favor each. Here is a review of that list, beginning with the seed we find successful in most yards.

Since day one, we have recommended, without qualification, black oil sunflower seeds, those little fellows that usually sell for something less than $12 per 50 pounds. The Audubon list shows 22 birds common to this area that will eat this seed. It is the favored seed of Northern Cardinals, Black-capped Chickadees, Evening Grosbeaks, House and Purple Finches, White-breasted and Red-breasted Nuthatches and White-throated Sparrows. Other birds that will eat black oil sunflower seeds include Blue Jays, Dark-eyed Juncos, American Goldfinches, Common Redpolls, Mourning Doves, Red-winged Blackbirds, Song Sparrows and all local woodpeckers except Pileated. Black oil is a sure bet. Put it on tray feeders or in tubes or your fly-through feeders. Scatter it on the ground. You can't go wrong.

Striped sunflower seeds, the big ones, are the choice of jays and Red-bellied Woodpeckers. Other birds that will take them include cardinals, chickadees, grosbeaks, Common Grackles, House and Purple finches, House Sparrows, nuthatches and White-throated and White-crowned sparrows. Use the same feeders mentioned previously.

Sunflower chips, the no-muss, no-fuss choice (because they have no hulls), are favored by Pine Siskins, cowbirds, cardinals, chickadees, goldfinches, grackles, House Finches, Mourning Doves, blackbirds and a sparrow species or two. House Sparrows, guests you might not want, will eat chips; nothing is perfect. Chips are best fed from feeders that will keep them from getting wet and clumping up. A tube or roofed feeder will work just fine.

Thistle, those thin little seeds that look like nothing at all, will appeal to goldfinches, Pine Siskins, redpolls, House and Purple finches, House Sparrows, doves, juncos and a sparrow species or two. Thistle takes a special tube feeder; ask the experts at your local wild bird supply store about this.

Cracked corn will please jays, thrashers, cardinals, juncos, bluebirds, grackles, House Sparrows, Mourning Doves, Red-bellied Woodpeckers, blackbirds, Rock Doves (pigeons), European Starlings, American Tree Sparrows, White-throated Sparrows and Mallards. Toss it on the ground or on an open platform feeder.

Peanuts in the shell? Certainly, say jays, woodpeckers and crows. The jays will be the first to take the peanuts, cleaning out whatever you offer by the end of the day. They cache a surplus against future procurement problems. Put the peanuts on a tray feeder. If you want to shell those peanuts, or buy shelled nuts, you can attract jays, nuthatches, chickadees, woodpeckers and the interlopers of the backyard, House Sparrows and European Starlings.

One benefit of feeding safflower seeds is that several creatures tend *not* to eat them: squirrels (which usually eat anything in your feeder and then the feeder itself), grackles and blackbirds. It will be taken by jays, cardinals, chickadees, House Finches, House Sparrows, doves, White-breasted Nuthatches and Red-bellied Woodpeckers. Put this in a tube feeder.

The bottom line: Black oil sunflower seed has about twice the drawing power of any other seed when the number of species attracted is the consideration. But, variety is good, too–more feeders and different foods will increase the appeal of your feeding efforts. More is better.

Recent additions to available seed choices include mixes that contain pieces of dried fruit. Some birds eat fruit, so this can expand your feeder potential. You can also add the fruit yourself; chopped raisins are an easy ingredient.

Don't forget suet. Birds that eat insects eat suet. It is a favored food in the winter when insects are hard to find.

Offer the birds water. Keep feeders clean. Keep them full. And, please, keep your cat indoors if you feed birds. — *Jim Williams*

birdfeeding–general

What birds can one expect to attract to feeders in the north central parts of the United States?

It depends on the landscape around you, how many feeders you use, what you put in the feeders and the time of year. Let's assume you're in a neighborhood with mature trees and shrubs, you have one feeder and feed a grocery-store mix. You are likely to see House Sparrows, Blue Jays, European Starlings, House Finches, Black-capped Chickadees, Northern Cardinals, White-breasted Nuthatches and American Goldfinches, among others. Add a suet feeder and you can attract Downy and Hairy woodpeckers and perhaps a Red-bellied Woodpecker. Buy the best feeder seed–black oil sunflower seed–and you'll discourage the two nuisance species (House Sparrows and starlings) and encourage more of the others. Put out more feeders and you'll attract more birds.

Why don't I have any birds at my feeders?

There are many reasons why some years produce lots of birds while others seem to have very few. To begin with, let's make a couple of assumptions. First, we'll assume that you are keeping your feeders filled on a regular basis. You don't let your feeders stand empty for days and days at a time. Birds have tiny brains, but they're very skilled at finding food. They know where it is and they know where it isn't. Second, we'll assume that you keep your cat indoors all of the time and your neighbors do likewise. Cats and birds mix in the worst possible way.

Now to the influences of Mother Nature: a good nesting season in the spring can produce an explosion of birds of many species in the fall and winter. A poor nesting season gives the opposite result.

A good food crop in the woods and parks near your house will tend to draw birds away from your feeders. Mild winters can do the same thing. The birds can find food without having to congregate at feeding stations.

A very cold snap in November or early December tends to push out the species that usually linger or attempt to overwinter. If this is followed by a warm spell in early winter, the northern species which normally move south may have no reason to do so–at least not during the early part of the winter.

Questions and Answers

Q: I'm wondering about the impact of banners, flags and whirligigs in the vicinity of birdfeeders. Will such things keep birds away?

A: Yes, they may; you can, in fact, use those very items to keep birds out of a yard or away from a house. If you want to attract birds, keep distractions to a minimum.

Q: Will wind chimes near my birdfeeder discourage birds from coming to the feeder?

A: Not unless it physically interferes with their feeding activity.

Q: We recently moved to a suburban townhouse. The yard has few trees, mostly very small. Are birdfeeders worth the effort here?

A: Yes, if you are willing to be patient. You need not wait for the trees to mature. Try seed on the ground. Try an open platform feeder. Try a birdbath or, better yet, moving water of some kind (a fountain or misting device). As always, the more dense vegetation you can add, the better.

Q: What can I plant to attract a larger variety of birds to my small city yard?

A: Trees that bear fruit, berries or cones are good. Choose varieties that offer food sources for several months. Select shrubs or trees that are native to the state, or at least native to North America. (We suggest native species specifically because introduced species often cause problems. They can be invasive, replacing native plants.) Aim at species which also provide good cover. Good summer plants might be Canada Plum, Common Chokecherry, Highbush Cranberry, Black or Red Raspberry and American Elderberry. For winter birds, cedar trees are good (Eastern Red Cedar is a favorite), as are Hackberry, Hawthorn, Glossy Black Chokecherry, Juneberry and Nannyberry. Birds need cover, good places to hide and roost, so your selections can help you in two ways. Thick bushes, cedar trees and conifers will help bring birds in. Remember that birds want enough openness to see where they are, to be able to watch for predators. Birds might avoid a yard boxed in with heavy vegetation, solid fences, a garage and the house.

Should I feed birds garden slugs that have drowned in stale beer? (Note: a saucer of stale beer placed in a garden is a common way to eliminate slugs.)

It probably wouldn't be a problem for the birds, but we don't recommend it. Few birds, if any, would eat them.

How can I attract goldfinches to my yard? I do have House Finches coming to my thistle seed feeders.

Feeder placement, surrounding habitat, the kind of feeders you use, the feed you use–all of these factors determine the kinds and numbers of birds at your feeders. Goldfinches will visit a variety of feeder types, but they seem to prefer hanging tube feeders. Place the feeders where they can easily be seen, are protected from the weather and away from routine people traffic. Keep the feeders clean and filled; don't let them go empty for even a day. Then, be patient. Birds come and go.

We have Mourning Doves that appear to be nesting in a grove of trees near our home. We want to keep these birds nearby. What can we feed them to bring them to our yard?

Mourning Doves will eat black oil sunflower seeds and millet. They prefer to feed on the ground or on open platform feeders very close to the ground.

If I fill my Droll Yankee feeder and leave the tray at the bottom empty I seem to get many fewer birds than if I also fill that tray. Why does that happen?

Without knowing exactly what you are feeding or what birds are coming to the feeder, we venture this comment: Some species might not be able to easily feed from the feeder ports. Some birds might not recognize the feed inside the feeder. Seed left on the tray at the bottom of your feeder is more visible and accessible.

How can I attract Pine Siskins and Common Redpolls to my feeders?

These birds are irregular visitors south of the Canadian border and their numbers vary from winter to winter. To bring them to your yard when they are in the area, offer Nyger thistle seed in a thistle feeder. Try peanut hearts and sunflower chips in a cylinder feeder with the larger feeding ports. Offer black oil sunflower seed and sunflower hearts and parts as well. Keep the feeder ports free of snow and ice.

Recently, I saw six robins in my backyard. I wondered if there was a special feed I could put out for them. I have suet and birdseed out there, but they don't seem to be interested in that.

American Robins generally won't come to suet or seed feeders. During the winter, they're surviving on berries and fruit–apples, crab apples, grapes, Mountain Ash berries, sumac berries and other such things. Try planting Red Splendor Crab, Prairie Fire Crab or Mountain Ash trees. Robins will eat cornbread, popcorn, raisins, peanut butter, apple slices and grape jelly. Offer this on a tray feeder. If you want to go to a pet shop and buy meal worms, you might find yourself a real robin hero. Meal worms are easy to raise if you want to have the most complete birdfeeder menu in the neighborhood.

Does birdfeeding change the distribution of birds?

The Mourning Dove, Northern Cardinal, Red-bellied Woodpecker and Tufted Titmouse are birds which have extended their range northward, perhaps due in part to feeding stations. Other environmental changes might be influencing northward movement of these species. The titmouse, for example, has been said to be expanding its range to the north because of birdfeeders. In Minnesota, however, the titmouse range has been shrinking southward. It was more common 50 years ago.

I put out birdfeeders in the winter for variety of birds. I feel at a certain point in the spring I should take the feeders down, that there is enough natural food for the birds. Is this a wise decision or should I maintain my feeders all year long?

If you want the birds to come to your yard for food throughout the year, keep the feeders in place and filled. It does no harm to feed during the warm months. In fact, some of the most interesting and colorful birds are here only in the summer–Indigo Bunting, Rose-breasted Grosbeak and

Baltimore Oriole. If you feed during migration periods and the breeding season, you are likely to see a wider variety of species at your feeders. When young birds have left the nest, you can also enjoy seeing juvenile birds in their particular plumages. Do check your feeders for mold and spoiling more often in warmer months, and clean your feeders more often.

I have read that feeding in the summer is a bad idea because the birds eat too much fat and may develop heart trouble. Is that true?

No. If you ate like a bird (worms and seed) your chances of heart trouble would probably be smaller.

Will feeding birds in the fall discourage migrants from leaving and cause them problems when the weather worsens?

Birds will migrate when it is time and they are ready to go. Providing food will help some species build the energy reserve needed for migration. Even offering the finest feast those birds ever saw would not convince them to overstay their schedule. Birds are not like the proverbial brother-in-law.

Are we interfering with nature when we feed wild birds?

It is estimated that birds coming to feeders take no more than 20 percent of their daily food requirement from such offerings. Besides, we interfere with the natural course of birds' lives far more by destroying habitat, building houses with glass windows, erecting high signal transmission towers, allowing cats to run free—you get the idea.

birdfeeding–food

How should I store my birdseed? Is it okay to leave it in the house?

Don't keep it in the house. The eggs, larva or adults of a nasty species of meal moth can be in the feed, best efforts of your bird store owner notwithstanding. If this critter hatches and gets loose in your house you will have a major problem. They are extraordinarily hard to eliminate once established. Keep the seed in a closed metal container, like a garbage can and store it in your garage.

Does the birdseed we buy to feed our birds contain pesticide or herbicide residue?

Farmers might use chemicals while the crop is being grown, as is the case with much of the food grown for human consumption. Are chemicals added during seed processing? Perhaps, usually to counter insect infestation and improve shelf life. It depends upon the company doing the processing. Ask your seed vendor about the practices of his or her suppliers.

The supermarket where we shop sells birdseed for much less than the seed at our local wild bird store. Is it a good deal?

This is a hard question to answer because much depends on the birds you can and/or seek to attract to your yard. In the past, grocery stores often carried very cheap seed mixes that tended to contain a lot of millet. This kind of seed is most popular with nuisance birds like House Sparrows, European Starlings and Common Grackles. Today, grocery stores often carry better seed selections. Check the contents list on the label of the seed bag, or simply take a good look at the seed in the bag. The best all-purpose seed you can buy, regardless of its source, is black oil sunflower. If you want to vary the offering, add striped sunflower, hulled sunflower (sometimes called parts and hearts), safflower, peanut kernels and Nyger thistle. Avoid rape seed, oats, hulled wheat and milo, simply because so few birds will take them. Watch the millet content (small round seeds); this seed is not high on most birds' preferred menu either. Discuss this with the owner of your local wild bird supply store. Describe your yard, your feeder setup and the birds you hope to attract. Ask for a seed recommendation.

What is a good bird feed?

Black oil sunflower is probably the best single food for your backyard birds. Nearly all feeder species will eat it, more than any other feeder food. It should make up 75 percent of all the feed you put out. If possible, use a few different kinds of feed at widely spaced feeders. Don't ask the birds to crowd together. This can spread disease. Unflavored suet in a wire cage nailed to a tree or hung from a branch is good. For the finches, try Nyger thistle in a feeder designed for that seed; ask your retailer. Peanuts will attract many interesting birds. Smaller birds like hulled sunflower hearts and sunflower chips. Hearts and parts, as some call it, can be very good if you have feeders on your deck or patio because there is less mess (shells) to clean up. However, these shelled seeds absorb moisture easily and can get moldy. Dump wet or moldy seed. It can cause disease in birds. Safflower seed is good because House Sparrows and European Starlings won't eat it and neither will squirrels. Oranges, apples and peanut butter will also attract some birds.

Will birds eat table scraps?

Not all of the scraps, but some birds and your dog might make a good team. You can offer the birds stale bread and baked goods, but this kind of food is likely to attract nuisance birds like House Sparrows and European Starlings. If you consider dried seeds from squash and pumpkins as scraps, offer those, too. Give the meat trimmings and leftover vegetables to Fido, not Tweety.

Is it okay to feed popped, stale popcorn to the birds in my yard?

Yes, Brown Thrashers love popcorn. But don't make it a regular thing. If you have leftover popcorn, no problem. But if you're thinking of using it as your main birdfood offering, add food items that are more attractive and nutritious such as black oil sunflower and other seeds.

Do birds eat acorns?

Blue Jays, White-breasted Nuthatches, Downy and Hairy Woodpeckers, Northern Flickers, Wood Ducks and Mallards are some of the species that enjoy acorns.

If I grow sunflowers in my garden, will birds eat the seeds that those plants produce?

Some of the same birds that take sunflower seeds from your feeders will eat directly from the seedhead on the plant. American Goldfinches, in particular, will favor wild sunflowers if you grow them in your garden. Let the complete plant stand through the winter.

Is it alright for me to scatter feed for the birds right on the ground?

Some birds prefer to find their food on the ground. Our native sparrow species (not House Sparrow) and juncos are more likely to ground feed than attend your mounted feeders. Clear away the snow and scatter the seed. In the spring, when migrating sparrows are moving through this area, build a small brush pile near your feeding spot. It will help attract birds.

Do birds ever need salt like deer and other mammals?

Yes. Their internal chemistry requires salt. Birds differ in their tolerance to salt; small amounts can be lethal to some species. Finches such as Evening Grosbeaks and crossbills, on the other hand, have a well-known appetite for salt. Crows, jays and White-Breasted Nuthatches have been observed consuming salt. Birds get the salt they need from natural sources. You need not offer it to birds as you might to deer.

I give my parakeet a little bit of grit every few days. I understand this helps the bird digest its food. Do wild birds need grit? Should I be putting this out on my feeders?

Wild birds do need grit (sand or small bits of gravel) of some kind. Usually, birds have no trouble finding enough. You can put it on your feeder tray if you wish, or mix it with the feed. A little will do.

What's the best treat I could give the birds in my yard for the holidays?

Here is a chance to be generous without busting your budget. Peanut butter is nice; buy a generic brand. The rib cage from the deer your brother-in-law shot, once cleaned of meat, will be a big hit. Chickadees, nuthatches and woodpeckers (and crows) will pick at the remaining scraps of meat and fat for months. Hang it (inconspicuously) from a tree branch. Suet is good. It need not have little seeds stuck in it. Here's a recipe: Mix one cup each of peanut butter, melted suet, peanut hearts, small raisins, flour and sunflower chips, with four cups of yellow cornmeal. Pack the mix (granular but sticky) into 1" holes drilled in a piece of wood and hang from a tree branch.

Are citrus fruit seeds good to feed to birds, squirrels or other wildlife?

No. There is little if any nutritional value in the seeds. There are other kitchen seeds which can be used. Northern Cardinals, for example, will eat seeds from cantaloupe, pumpkin, squash and watermelon. Orange halves will attract Baltimore and Orchard Orioles, Red-headed Woodpeckers and Red-bellied Woodpeckers. Warblers and orioles will eat bananas (sliced the long way). Raisins and dried currants will be taken by bluebirds, catbirds, mockingbirds, robins, tanagers, thrashers, cardinals and White-crowned Sparrows. And as long as you're in the kitchen fixing bird lunch, consider peanut butter, dried apples, broken walnuts and peanuts. Soak dried fruit in water before putting it out. To present these items, just scatter them on a tray feeder or other flat surface.

What happens to the birds at my feeder if I have to go away for a week or two?

If the feeders run dry, the birds will find food elsewhere. They will take you off their food route. When you again fill the feeders, be patient. Eventually, the birds will return. If you have someone watch the house in your absence, ask them to fill the feeders for you.

Do birds eat salted peanuts?

Yes, but unless your birds are into beer and football, you need not buy salted peanuts. Save money by going to your neighborhood wild bird supply store and buying shelled peanuts that have been rejected for human use but are perfectly suitable for wildlife. That store is likely to have a shelled-peanut feeder as well, unless you want to fashion your own from quarter-inch hardware cloth. Birds which will feed on peanuts include Blue Jays, White-breasted Nuthatches, cardinals, Black-capped Chickadees, several sparrow species and all of our woodpeckers except Pileated. Blue Jays will readily take peanuts in the shell.

birdfeeding–suet

Will I attract insects and other pests if I put suet out for the birds? Does suet smell bad in warm weather?

Suet maintains its integrity well in all but the hottest weather when direct sunlight will cause it to soften or melt. Suet could attract a few flies but probably not enough to be troublesome and odor should not be a problem. It is a good idea to trim any meat from the suet before putting it outside. That should help keep odor to a minimum. Raccoons, bears and squirrels will come to suet. Some of us consider them pests. Use hardware cloth to completely enclose your suet and attach the suet container firmly to a tree or post. This will discourage the animals and keep them from dragging your feeder into the brush. If you have bear problems, the best solution is to take the suet down until the bears leave the neighborhood.

Questions and Answers

My neighbor said I could take the rib cage from the deer I shot and hang it in my yard for the birds. Is that true?

Birds will eat the bits of meat and fat left on the bones. Chickadees, Blue Jays, woodpeckers and crows will clean up those ribs and they won't ask for barbecue sauce.

If I put bacon fat in my suet feeder, will birds eat it?

Most birds that take suet also take bacon fat or melted fat from beef, pork, veal, lamb or poultry. Heat the fat to remove excess moisture, strain it and store it in the refrigerator or freezer. It is best used by mixing it with other ingredients, as in suet cakes, instead of placing the meat fat in the holder by itself. Bacon or meat fat will be more likely to melt and run in direct sunlight or hot weather than will suet.

Can you offer recipes for suet mixes to be fed to birds this winter?

Here are two variations on that theme. The first is made from one cup of peanut butter, one cup of vegetable shortening, melted beef suet or bacon drippings, four cups of yellow cornmeal and one cup of white flour. This makes a soft, doughy food. Place it in your suet feeder, a nylon mesh bag, or roll it into balls and simply place on your platform feeder. A second recipe calls for four cups of yellow cornmeal, one cup all-purpose flour, one cup lard or melted grease/suet and one teaspoon corn oil. When this is mixed, stir in sunflower hearts, peanut hearts or chopped raisins (or all three). Offer it to the birds as described above. These are best used in cold months since animal fats (but not suet) melt in the sun of warmer seasons.

Can I simply put suet chunks on top of our platform-style birdfeeder or does it have to be in one of those wire holders?

Squirrels and crows could carry off your suet if it is not contained somehow. Buy a wire-mesh holder or build one yourself of ½" mesh hardware cloth. Use a mesh onion bag.

birdfeeding–feeders

Q: Where can I find sources of plans for building birdfeeders?

A: Check with your local bird store, book store or library. There are several good books available. The web site of the North American Bluebird Society also has good nest box information. That address is www.nabluebirdsociety.org. One of the best books is *Woodworking for Wildlife*, published by the Minnesota Department of Natural Resources.

Q: I see feeders for sale that attach to a window with suction cups. Will birds actually come that close to my house? Will the feeder lure them into collision with the window glass?

A: Birds will use these feeders, giving you and your family a nose-to-beak view of your visitors. Feeders placed that close to the window glass produce few if any window strikes; birds are simply too close to the glass to fly into it. The birds have to fly away from the glass to leave. These feeders are recommended for reducing window mortality.

Q: My wooden birdfeeders are old and coming apart. Does this discourage birds from using them? Should I buy new feeders?

A: Birds are easy to please. One of the best sets of feeders we've seen was roughly built and unpainted but exceptionally successful because of what was on the feeders and where they were placed. The birds want food. If mold and rot is invading cracks and crevices on your feeders, a renewal program would be a good idea. You want to keep the feeders clean and free of mold, fungus and rot.

Q: I put bird feed on the ground in my yard, but in the winter the snow always covers it up. Is it okay to build a roof over the feed to keep the snow off? Will this scare the birds away?

A: A roof or lean-to arrangement is just fine for your feeding area. Be sure to leave the birds an easy and clear entrance and exit. Be certain the birds will not be slowed in their escape if predators find them.

How high off the ground should my birdfeeders be?

About half of the birds which commonly come to feeders will prefer a height of no more than 6' off the ground. The others, including finches, will like it higher and away from yard activity. Try putting your finch feeders (thistle seed) higher, the others lower.

Are metal perches on birdfeeders too cold for birds' feet in winter?

Birds have little fleshy muscle and relatively few nerve endings in their feet. Consequently, they are less likely to experience discomfort from cold or heat. Birds do occasionally lose a toe or even an entire foot to injury by freezing (more likely because the foot became wet), but casual observation indicates that this seldom happens.

Do I need to clean my birdfeeder?

Yes. Birdfeeders need periodic maintenance, at the very least in the fall and spring. Dirty feeders breed disease. Don't invite birds to a meal which will make them sick. Scrape the accumulated gunk from feeder trays and platforms. If possible, wash the feeder in hot soapy water. Really clean it. Allow it to thoroughly dry in the sun before refilling with seed. Do this three or four times a year. It also helps if you simply remove seed hulls and residue from your feeders each time you replace the seed.

Water for Birds

Feeders bring wild birds into your yard. Water will do the same. If you have feeders, giving birds a supply of water for drinking and bathing could make a significant difference in the both the number of birds you see and the different species attracted.

Water can work magic.

In each of our first two suburban yards, my wife Jude and I built simple and inexpensive pools or fountains that added much to our birding pleasure. We moved last winter. Plans are in place for construction of a third pool at our new location.

The first pool–and that is an ambitious word to describe a watering hole as small as this one–was an oval about the size of a bath mat, 12" deep. A thin coating of concrete gave it permanent shape and sealed it from leakage. We placed rocks at its edges to give birds access to the water. When evaporation lowered the level, we turned on the garden hose and added water.

This pool, placed in the middle of a shady wildflower garden, worked well. Frogs came. Mallards came. And so did many neighborhood birds. Because the water was stagnant, however, it fouled in warm weather. It required regular attention. Sometimes it had to be bailed dry, cleaned and refilled.

In the second yard, we constructed a similar pool, perhaps 4' by 2', varying in depth from 1" to 18". We improved on our first idea by buying a very simple fountain. It stood on a narrow pole pedestal close beside the pond. A small hose ran from the fountain head down inside the pedestal and to an outside faucet at the back of the house. We buried the thin plastic tube which carried the water from the faucet. The faucet was turned on just enough to produce a trickle of water.

The water burbled from the fountain head, filled a shallow plate at the top of the pedestal, then dripped into the pool below. On a quiet evening you could hear the pleasant sound of falling water. We could control the speed and quantity of water by a very slight turn of the faucet handle.

The constant input of fresh water kept this pool from going sour. It remained fresh and full from spring to freeze-up. We were even able to grow water plants there. We simply placed them in the deepest part of the pool, leaving the plants in the nursery containers in which we bought them.

Birds routinely bathed and drank in both the shallow plate at the top of the fountain and in the pool below. Cardinals came. Rose-breasted Grosbeaks brought their youngsters. Baltimore Orioles used the pool. Catbirds came from the thicket behind the house to drink. Mourning Doves stood in the evening shade at the pool's edge, tipping forward to take water, tipping upright to swallow, back and forth like little toys. Chipmunks and squirrels drank there, as did the neighborhood woodchuck and one of its offspring. Canada Geese stopped by. We had more Mallard visitors.

Birds that did not come to eat at our feeders came to drink and bathe in the water. A significant part of the attraction here was the moving water. The sound and motion helped catch the bird's attention. We were advertising.

As you might expect, the plan for pool number three is more elaborate. We're going to dig a much larger hole, but not deeper. Birds prefer shallow depths, an inch or two giving them all the water they need. Songbirds, after all, don't have long legs.

What we seek this time is a meandering pool nestled at the foot of a rock retaining wall already in place. The plan has another hose running from the house to the pool. Water will be pumped to the top of the retaining wall, to cascade down a small waterfall we hope will serve as our advertising. The pond will have a lower end from which excess water will drain onto tolerant plants.

We're buying supplies for this pool–a waterproof liner and a small electric pump chief among them. There is talk of a small bridge. The pool will become part of a shady garden area. But its foremost purpose will be to bring more birds to the yard.

We have a friend who built a magnificent waterfall in his very tiny backyard, in a neighborhood of tiny backyards. His waterfall sits on no more than two square yards of ground. It has four levels. Water recirculates, via a pump, from bottom to top. In the spring, he tells us, migrant warblers stop to drink and bathe there. Throughout the warm season, his yard is a bird haven. He says the water does it.

I have never tried to keep my pools open in the winter. I certainly wouldn't expect to keep a large pool free of ice. But electric heaters are available that will keep an ordinary birdbath open in the winter, allowing birds to find the water they need in all seasons. — *Jim Williams*

birds and water

How do you clean birdbaths?

Cleaning your birdbaths several times a season is a good idea. Clean it with a good detergent and a stiff brush, assuming these won't damage the surface of the bowl. Make certain you rinse the bowl well before refilling it. Do your cleaning away from the area where you feed birds.

What do birds do for water in the winter?

They get it where they can find it. Birds eat snow, look for puddles of melting snow or find a birdbath that is being kept open. A heated birdbath can be very successful in attracting birds in the winter. You can prevent the water from freezing with a special electric heating element (available at your local bird store). Some birdbaths now come with built-in heaters. You should pay close attention to the amount of water in your container, since dry winter air will cause accelerated evaporation.

I bought a birdbath heater this winter and am using it. We have a chain-link fence around our yard. Twice I have found birds frozen to our fence. Is this a problem I can solve or just bad luck for the birds?

You can solve this problem. Water for birds in the winter should be for drinking, not bathing. Cover your birdbath with a wire mesh such as hardware cloth (ask your hardware dealer) that allows the birds to drink but not bathe. Another option is to cover the birdbath with thin boards, leaving narrow channels through which the birds can drink. Most native birds won't bathe during temperatures that are below freezing. European Starlings are one species that will. They are an exotic (non-native) species that has not yet learned to avoid bathing in cold weather.

housing

Nest Boxes

If you want to attract nesting birds with nesting boxes, those small structures known as bird houses, you have to play by the birds' rules.

A friend of mine was given a dozen bluebird nest boxes by a man who had volunteered to build them for a local project. My friend was to put them in place on the grounds of a museum. No big deal.

In the builder's garage he found a very large collection of nest boxes destined to be ignored and empty forever, no matter where you might put them.

What was wrong?

The boxes were the wrong size for the birds intended. The entry holes were the wrong size. The boxes had perches. They were screwed tightly together, top, bottom and on all four sides, impossible to conveniently open if you wanted to check on the nesting bird or clean the box.

The problem was, this guy was not the Lone Ranger of bird boxes. He has lots of company, much of it commercial.

Let's start with perches. Cavity nesters–and a nesting box is simply an artificial cavity–don't need perches. Many of these birds nest in holes created by woodpeckers in trees or posts. Have you ever seen a woodpecker install a perch by drilling a tiny hole and jamming in a short twig?

Perches are welcomed only by predators. The structures give them assistance as they stick their paws into the nest box to grab and eat eggs and nestlings.

A hole in a tree, which basically is what you are building or buying when you offer nest boxes, is a simple but specific thing.

Briefly, birds want a nest box of the correct size and material in the correct place. Floor space is important. The size of the hole is critical, both for allowing entry of the nesting bird and keeping nest box competitors (think starlings and House Sparrows) out. Placement of the box is important, including height from the ground. You cannot build or buy just any box, not if you want to be successful.

The guy with the garage filled with poorly designed houses is spreading failure. If you put up a nest box and birds ignore it, what happens? The birds lose a nesting opportunity and worse, you lose interest.

Not every nest box, no matter how well designed and how well placed, will attract nesting birds. Territorial demands, food and water supply and predators (cats!), all play a role. But you can create short odds for yourself by paying attention to what birds want.

April is the time to put up nest boxes. Depending on your yard, you can provide nesting quarters for chickadees, nuthatches, woodpeckers, House Wrens, bluebirds and Tree Swallows, among other species. Wood ducks will use boxes, as will some owls. It all depends on the particular box and habitat in which you place it, be it your yard or at your cabin or at Uncle John's.

Visit with the experts at your neighborhood wild bird store. Ask questions. Understand the answers. Buy a book. Follow directions. This can be an entertaining and rewarding project. Share it with a child; that makes it even better.

And, on a personal note, I believe cute is a puppy, not a bird house. I avoid nesting boxes with chimneys, shutters, a bench on the porch and little flowers painted around the (excuse the expression) door. — *Jim Williams*

nesting birds

Will birds use donated materials like thread and string to build their nests?

Yes. In the spring some folks hang short pieces of such material, including dog hair, in their yards for birds to take and use in nest building. Somber, natural colors seem to be more frequently used than bright colors. Blue Jays will sometimes incorporate pieces of paper in their nests. Robins might include a bit of rag. Baltimore Orioles will use yarn or string. And House Sparrows will completely jam a bird house with a truly amazing collection of all of these things and more.

Can you tell by looking at a bird's nest which species built the nest or do they pretty much all look alike?

All bird species build identifiable nests. In some cases, clues come from the method of construction. The hanging, pendulum-like nest of Baltimore Orioles is a good example. In other cases, construction material might lead you to the identity of the builder. Placement is also a key. Tree Swallows build in cavities (nest boxes or holes in trees), and almost always weave a feather or two into the grass nest. Song Sparrows line their cup-like nests with fine grasses or hair.

I have built some bird houses and was thinking of painting them. Will paint make any difference to the birds?

It should make little or no difference to the birds. Don't use wood that has been treated with preservatives. Use no creosote. If you must, paint only the outside of the house with a color that blends with the landscape.

Is it necessary to remove old bird nests from nesting boxes before a new nesting season begins? Will birds reuse old nests or build over them?

It is best to remove old nests and clean out the box. Bluebirds sometimes build atop an old nest, but removing old nests is a good idea. Be careful when you do this. Wear gloves and wet the nest with a disinfectant spray before taking it out. Don't breathe the dust that might arise. Bag the old nest and put it in the garbage. The danger here is possible mouse droppings, a known source of sometimes serious human disease. Also watch for wasps nesting beneath the box. Sounds pretty serious, doesn't it? Well, don't lose sleep over it, but do be careful.

Questions and Answers

When should bird houses be cleaned of old nesting material?

Before the birds want to use the house again. For Eastern Bluebirds, clean the box as soon as the young leave the nest. Wood Duck nesting boxes are best cleaned in the fall, when the nesting season is over. Do not disturb active nests unless you have House Sparrows. If you are certain the birds are House Sparrows and you wish to discourage this non-native species in its competition with native birds, remove the nest and eggs and continue to do so if the House Sparrows nest again.

If I put up bird houses in my yard, how can I be sure that those houses are what the birds want to use?

You need the right house in the right place. Many species you see in your yard are cavity nesters, responding well to nesting houses since there is always a shortage of good natural cavities. Again, get good advice about which bird house is correct for the species you wish to attract and where you should place the house. Talk to an expert.

I have purchased a birch-bark bird house, shaped like a teepee, with a 1" entry hole. Will birds use this house?

Maybe. 1" is acceptable for House Wrens, but chickadees need a minimum hole size of 1⅛". Birds nesting in cavities (those are the species that would use your house) have particular needs in regard to size of cavity, size of entry hole and location. Stay away from gimmick houses. Buy bird houses from someone who knows what they are selling.

In May we had a Purple Finch build its nest by our porch light. In July, the finches were building again and laid one egg in the nest. Did the bird nest for a second time or is this one of the young from the first nest?

This surely is a House Finch, because Purple Finches do not nest on light fixtures. It could be a second brood by your original nester. But it is not the nest of a youngster from that first family. Those birds will not breed until next spring.

Last year a House Finch nested on our condo balcony. Should I take the old nest down this year or leave it up?

Most birds do not reuse nests, so take the old nest down. This might even encourage renesting in the same general area. Remove the old nest carefully, perhaps immediately putting it into a paper bag. Bird nests can be very dusty and dirty, often containing insects.

As a youth I built wren houses readily used by those birds. I have put up pine wren houses in my yard now but have no wrens. Why not?

It is probably a habitat issue. House Wrens prefer brushy, weedy habitat and the edges of wooded areas. Houses should be 5-10' off the ground, on a tree or under the eaves of a building. Wren houses also can be hung, the only kind of nest box you can place in that fashion. The entrance hole should be 1⅛" in diameter. Do not put a perch below the hole (never put perches on nest boxes for any bird).

Why did the female House Wren in our yard have nests in two houses last year and appear to be flying back and forth between them? It seemed the males were sitting on the eggs. Do male birds do that?

Male and female House Wrens look alike. The bird flying from nest to nest was most likely the male. He started two nests or perhaps as many as half a dozen in his efforts to define and defend his territory. The males also pilfer sticks from the nests of competitors or destroy those nests. The female wren then chooses one nest in which to lay eggs, announcing her intentions by placing the final lining in the selected nest. The female might also have added a few sticks or twigs to the nest if she felt the male didn't build to her standards. The male does not help with incubation, but occasionally brings food to the female.

I had House Wrens nesting in my yard last summer for the first time. Is the same pair of birds likely to return here and nest again next spring?

Some birds will return to the same nesting box. Banding studies have shown this to be true of Eastern Bluebirds. If one pair of wrens chose your nesting box, chances are it will be used again. We just can't say for certain that your former tenants will return.

Questions and Answers

When do House Wrens return in the spring and begin to nest? Can I attract them to my yard with food or nesting boxes? How long does it take wren eggs to hatch? How many young do wrens have?

House Wrens return to the upper Midwest from mid-April to mid-May. Males will begin building more than one nest, a means of marking territory boundaries and attracting a mate. The males allow the female to choose the nest she prefers for her eggs, which hatch in 12-14 days. Young birds will leave the nest in about another two weeks. Wrens are insect eaters, hard birds to provide feed for. You can, however, provide meal worms in a small dish; see your local wild bird store about this. You would most likely have better luck attracting them by providing housing; wrens readily use bird houses. Talk to the folks at your local bird store about appropriate house size and placement, both important factors.

Both my neighbor and I had wrens nesting in houses in our yards this year. Should we clean houses this fall, when nesting is finished? What height is best for these houses?

Yes, you can clean them after nesting. The best bird houses allow you to easily remove a panel (assembled with screws) so you don't have to try to pull the sticks out through the entry hole. If you've ever watched a wren trying to push those sticks into the house you know the job you face trying to pull them out. Empty the house, give the insides a quick dusting to get rid of miscellaneous dirt, then reassemble and replace the house. A good height is 5-10' off the ground in an area with some cover. Don't put wren houses out in the open.

I hear Mourning Doves morning and night in and near our yard. Are they nesting here? Where would I look for the nest?

Mourning Doves–named for the mournful tone of their call–nest throughout the upper Midwest. Mourning Doves nest most often in trees or shrubs 10-25' off the ground, though they sometimes nest right on the ground. The nest is a thin, shallow platform of twigs, weed stems or grasses. The male gathers the nesting material and the female builds the nest. These doves will often nest more than once per season.

About Backyard Birds

Last summer a Mourning Dove built a nest on our condo patio and hatched three sets of babies. Is the same bird likely to return this year and reuse the nest? Should we let her do it?

The nesting pair of birds might come back. They are unlikely to use the same nest again. If they were no problem for you, welcome their return. Many birdwatchers would pay to have an easily observable nest in their yard.

Every summer, Killdeer attempt to nest on the ballfields in the park behind my yard and end up in conflict with ballplayers. What type of plants or other landscaping would you suggest to encourage Killdeer to nest in my backyard instead?

Killdeer like bare, open, rocky ground for nesting. You would not add plants to attract these birds. An isolated piece of bare ground, perhaps covered with gravel, might be attractive to these birds.

We have Black-capped Chickadees nesting beneath our window air conditioner. Does running the machine bother or endanger the birds or their nesting success? When we remove the air conditioner in the fall, do we need to worry about harming the nest?

If the birds are still there, they probably don't mind the noise. We have read of Purple Martins nesting inside the speaker cones of a city's emergency siren system. Those birds even fledged young, an occasional warning blast notwithstanding. And by the time you bring your air conditioner in for the season, the chickadees will be finished with nesting chores. Next year they will build anew.

We have a nest box in our yard. Chickadees used it last summer, raising two broods. They used it this past winter for shelter. We have not seen nesting activity in the house this spring. Is it necessary to clean the house for re-use? When? Is it too late now?

It is probably a good idea to clean out the house each fall. If you clean the house in the early summer you have a chance to attract birds attempting to raise a second, late-season brood. It certainly couldn't hurt to give it a try.

I would like to know why birds, especially robins, keep building nests on the light fixture outside my front door. I keep tearing the nest down. The birds keep rebuilding. There are trees in my yard, so why do they use the light fixture?

The birds probably found your light fixture to be the most suitable site for their nest. The fixture might appear to be better protected from predators, notably the raccoons and cats in your neighborhood. Both can climb trees. Another possibility is that there might be rival birds already nesting in your trees.

How can I attract nesting Purple Martins to my yard? Do swallows act as scouts for martins?

Swallows and martins have not made a deal. Purple Martins must find their own nesting locations. What they're looking for are cavities (nesting boxes will do just fine) in wide open grassy areas near water. If you have a martin house in a proper location, keep House Sparrows out of it by plugging the nest entrances until martins are present. Keep the nest box entrances sealed during the winter.

We have a Wood Duck house in a willow tree overlooking a small pond. Every year, the duck has used the nest but abandoned it without hatching ducklings. Can we make the house or nest more attractive to the bird? We have squirrels. Are they the problem?

The squirrels could be the problem. They'll readily move into duck boxes. Check also for European Starling nests. Raccoons could be raiding the nest. And check these basics: the house should be 15' or more off the ground, the entry hole oval, 3" high and 4" wide, facing water. Make sure there is a roughened area on the inside of the face board, below the hole, to give the ducklings a grip as they climb out of the nest. Add 4" of wood shavings or chain-saw chips (not sawdust) to the inside of the box when you prepare it.

baby birds

Last summer the House Wrens nesting in our yard fledged their young in early August. The small birds seemed to spend the next week or so hiding beneath bushes. This seems a high-risk way to begin life. Is this the normal way wrens do things?

You were watching very typical behavior for wrens and some other birds. The young leave the nest when they outgrow it. They must learn to fly by practicing, but cannot do so until their feathering is adequate for the job. The timing of all of these events can dictate some time on the ground.

We rescued a young robin that fell from its nest. Do we have to feed it worms? Will it eat other things?

You more than likely kidnapped that bird, not rescued it. There comes a time when young birds are supposed to leave the nest. Their parents continue to feed them at this time, even if they are no longer in or near the nest. While these birds look like helpless babies, they function well if left to the skills of their parents who know exactly what to feed them and how else to care for them. Occasionally, you may find a truly helpless young bird that has fallen from a nest. These birds will be downy or have undeveloped feathers. Find a wildlife rehabilitation center and ask for advice. If in doubt, put the bird back in the nest and leave the area.

Which robin removes fecal sacs (the droppings of the nestlings) from the nest, the male or the female?

It's a lot like changing diapers for human parents. The sac is usually removed by the bird that finds it first.

We often see baby robins. Why don't we ever see baby chickadees and cardinals?

You do see young chickadees and cardinals, you just don't recognize them as such. Baby robins have a plumage that looks different from that of adults. This species and others will achieve adult feathering at a later date, after molting that juvenile plumage. Young cardinals and chickadees are among those species which look much like their parents (the female in the case of the cardinal) once fledged. These birds undergo seasonal molts too, but exchange one set of adult feathers for another.

Questions and Answers

Q: **I enjoy watching pelicans near our lake home in the summer. I never see baby pelicans, though. Why not? Are they born elsewhere in the winter or what?**

A: American White Pelicans, the species seen in the upper Midwest, nest in large colonies. In the spring, these birds choose to nest on remote islands on large lakes where they will be undisturbed by people. While adult birds can range many miles from their nesting areas during the breeding season, the young birds stay in the colonies until they are perhaps ten weeks old. By then, they look much like their parents.

Q: **How long does it take a bird to hatch its eggs? How long does it take for the young to leave the nest after hatching? Are the young birds self-sufficient at that time?**

A: For each species the story is different. Black-capped Chickadees hatch eggs in 12 to 13 days and the young, born naked and helpless, leave the nest 16 days later, feathered and learning to fly. The young remain with the adults for another three to four weeks. Killdeer incubate their eggs for about 25 days. The young hatch as feathered, active birds, brooded and guarded by adults but able to feed themselves.

troubles

The Bear-proof Birdfeeder

One of the world's truly great birdfeeders was designed by a man living in Duluth, Minnesota. You probably didn't know that.

It was assembled to put an end to bears getting fat on black oil sunflower seed, likely not a problem in a suburban yard. But if it works for bears–and it does–it has a 50-50 chance of being effective against squirrels, which makes this important.

Our hero is named John Boynton. I met him when he came to remodel a house we had purchased in a very weak moment. He spent almost a year with us because the house needed much work. (That is another story, maybe a book and perhaps a movie.) Anyhow, if you hang around me long enough you can catch a serious birdfeeding virus. John did.

Before long he was arriving on the job at least one morning a week with a new birdfeeder to show me. John is a fine craftsman and clever, too. He gave us a series of mighty fine feeders, all of which drew birds like fleas to a dog.

Now our story moves to bear country. We spend some time in the woods where black bears are routinely seen. So does John.

That spring I heard too much noise on our bear-country deck. I walked to the living room window and looked for the source of the noise. It was out there, standing in front of the window, looking in. I don't know what the bear thought as he stared at me. What I thought was, hey, you see something in the yard that you like, go ahead, take it.

The bear did. It bent a 2" steel pipe to the ground, then ate several pounds of seed from the feeder which had been atop the pipe. It trashed the feeder for dessert. It knocked over and broke a second feeder. It tore down my super-large suet holder and took it away, perhaps as a souvenir. And it wrote down our address in its route book.

Our next meeting with Mr. Boynton, sometime after he had rebuilt our house, was in his woods, beneath a magnificent birdfeeding structure.

"It's bear-proof," John said with the pride of an artist. "Here, you can see the scratches the bear made when he tried to climb." Sure enough, big scratches, no damage.

John had bought a 13' long 3" steel pipe, setting 3' of it in the ground, encased in cement. Over the remaining 10' of pipe he slipped 4" PVC tubing, capping it with a four-way joint. To this he attached two smaller pieces of PVC as arms, you might say. From these arms, way, way up there, he hangs his feeders, tube feeders and homemade peanut feeders constructed of small-caliber hardware cloth. And, yes, he does use a ladder to fill the feeders.

The crowning touch here, literally, is a large wire basket placed as center-piece at the top of the pole. John fills that with suet. This is like the Eiffel Tower of birdfeeders, beautiful, white and trim, stylish even.

I built ours in similar fashion, though with less style, as soon as I could. I made one modification: to accommodate more feeders (more feeders, more birds) we have longer arms on ours. Jude, my birdfeeding partner, says it lends our yard a certain Easter quality.

What is important is we have lost no more feeders to bear attacks. None. Zip. Nada. No squirrels climb it, either. They don't even try. It is raccoon-proof as well, probably secure from all mammals but half a dozen African species.

A note about one other feeder I favor. This is one of those hot-wired jobs, two D batteries and some fancy electronics that produce a few volts when hind paws are on the feeder tray and little front paws are on a seed-port perch, as they would be if a squirrel were looking for bird food.

It does not take many volts to impress a squirrel. Three, two, one, zap! We have liftoff, Houston! Surprised squirrels leap from the feeder, furry missiles going amazing distances for such nonaerodynamic objects. They return to sniff at the feeder, raising their narrow noses to what used to be free lunch, but they don't try it a second time. — *Jim Williams*

mammals at feeders

I've noticed rabbits feeding beneath my birdfeeder. Is this unusual?

Not at all. The rabbits are taking advantage of your generosity. Many mammals eat at birdfeeders. The Eastern Gray Squirrel is probably the one you see most often. Red Squirrels, Southern Flying Squirrels, Raccoons, various mice, voles and shrews and White-tailed Deer are often found at urban feeders in this part of the country. Depending on location, feeders in the country can attract Pine Marten, Fisher, Northern Flying Squirrel, Virginia Opossum, Gray and Red Fox, Black Bear and Striped Skunk. The other common mammal at birdfeeders is the house cat. Enjoy the visits of the other creatures if you can, but don't let the cats near the birds. Keep your cat inside. Ask your neighbors to do the same.

How can I discourage cats from hunting around my feeders?

Determine who owns the cat and talk to that person. Ask that the cat be kept indoors. If the cat continues to be a nuisance, call your community animal control department. If cats aren't covered under animal-control ordinances, complain to the city council. The average life span of a cat allowed outdoors is significantly lower than that of an indoor-only cat. You are doing the cat, its owner and the birds a favor by convincing the owner to keep the animal confined. As a last resort, try squirting the cat with a large squirt gun filled with vinegar. Cats hate vinegar. Do remember, though, that your real problem is with the owner of the cat, not with the cat itself.

Last winter I found a series of small holes and tunnels in the snow under my birdfeeders. What is making these holes?

Meadow Voles and shrews, most likely. These small rodents probably consider your feeder the mother of all winter food sites. If you like drama, watch for visiting owls. They feed on rodents and sometimes adopt birdfeeders as, well, the mother of all winter food sites.

Questions and Answers

squirrels

Q. What can I do about all the squirrels at my feeders?

A. We might as well begin with this question, perhaps the number-one query among people who feed birds. And if you happen to not ask the question, you surely have an opinion about the answer. Some of us favor squirrel-free zones. Others firmly believe that all of Ma Nature's children have a place in the choir, and that includes squirrels. If you are so inclined, trapping problem squirrels is legal all year. Squirrels taken in a live trap can be relocated if you wish, but remember, this simply delivers the problem to someone else. A more effective solution is to put squirrel guards on your feeder posts. There are several commercial models available. Place the guard at least 3' off the ground. A 2' length of sheet metal stove pipe from the hardware store also works well. The pipe fits beneath the feeder, over the post. Cut tabs at one end of the pipe and nail them to the feeder.

Counter-balanced feeders that close the feeder ports when a squirrel positions itself to eat also work well. Another solution is to hang your feeders from wire strung between trees or a tree and the edge of your roof. The wire should be high enough so you don't walk into it and low enough so you can reach the feeder to fill it.

Also, keep your feeders at least 12' from the nearest tree, bush or other squirrel access. These critters can really jump, especially for a free lunch. Or you can be benevolent and put out additional food–usually cracked corn–for the squirrels. Establish this feeding area away from your birdfeeders.

Q. How can I keep squirrels out of my Wood Duck houses?

A. Isolate the house on a post, away from trees, with a predator guard of some kind installed on the post. A sheet-metal sheath covering about 2' of the post will keep most critters from climbing; grease the metal for more protection. The house has to be high enough, of course, to prevent successful leaping. You can also place the Wood Duck house in shallow water. This stops squirrels (but not raccoons). Trapping squirrels is another idea. Live-traps of various kinds can work well, but only move the problem elsewhere. Nuisance squirrels can legally be killed out of season if you have a special permit.

I read that you can put hot red pepper in birdseed to keep squirrels away. Is this true? Will the pepper hurt the birds?

A little cayenne pepper or the additive sold for this purpose in wild bird stores can be added to the seed you put in your feeders. It will not bother the birds. But users report mixed results with the squirrels. Sometimes, it doesn't bother them either.

We have an albino squirrel in our neighborhood. It seems to be intimidated by the Gray and Red squirrels. Why is the albino afraid of the others? Can albino squirrels mate with regular squirrels? Will the resultant litter be albino? How common are albinos? Are their life spans shorter than those of regular squirrels?

The squirrel's reaction to other squirrels probably is not related to its color but to its position in the hierarchy of the neighborhood squirrel population. New and young squirrels usually occupy the lowest rungs. Yes, albinos can mate with squirrels of regular color. Albino squirrels are not rare. Their life spans might be shorter simply because they are more noticeable to predators like cats or large owls. Black squirrels, incidentally, are at the other end of the color chart from albinos, exhibiting melanism, a high degree of pigmentation.

What kind of poison can I use on squirrels?

Do not poison squirrels. Poison is illegal for squirrels and almost without fail available to animals beyond the target species. You kill more broadly than you intend. Poisoned animals are often eaten by scavengers, both birds and mammals, including neighborhood dogs. The scavengers can then be affected by the poison. Squirrels also are a game species in most states. They are protected by specific rules for the season in which and method by which they can be taken. Talk to your bird supply retailer about squirrel control tactics.

Do squirrels eat bird eggs or young birds?

Yes. Eastern Chipmunks, and Gray and Red squirrels all will eat an occasional bird egg or nestling. The bulk of their food, however, is vegetable in nature.

Q: How can I keep the squirrels from eating the suet I put out for the birds?

A: The suet cages sold in bird or hardware stores should work. They hold the suet well for the birds while preventing squirrels and crows from making off with major chunks. You can fashion your own wire suet feeder with hardware cloth. Choose the ½" mesh. Also try hanging the suet from a feeder which is inaccessible to the squirrels.

Q: We are having trouble with our hanging seed feeder. We fill it in the morning and by the afternoon the squirrels and large birds have dumped the feed to the ground. We would prefer to feed the smaller birds, the chickadees, nuthatches and finches. What can we do?

A: You can try to hang the feeder where the squirrels cannot gain access. You can block access with a squirrel baffle, although these clever animals aren't always baffled by baffles. Larger birds pose another problem. You can buy feeders which are enclosed in wire mesh with openings large enough for small birds to enter but small enough to exclude birds the size of jays or blackbirds. You also can use a tube feeder designed strictly for dispensing Nyger thistle seed. This seed is readily taken by finches but generally not used by larger birds. If the feeder perches are made of wood or plastic, you might also clip them shorter, making it difficult for larger birds to perch there.

Crows

Somewhere to the south of us, early each spring, thousands of crows, hundreds of thousands of crows, are stretching their wings and preparing to move north for the summer. They will rejoin their overwintering brethren for our warm season.

The migrants are in Arkansas and Missouri and Iowa during the winter months, looking north, dreaming of early, early mornings in your yard, cawing and crowing and carrying on well before you plan to wake, plotting marauding mischief to fill their days and make yours anxious.

These crows know where you live. They recognize the curtains in your bedroom windows. They know which buttons to push to make your pulse rate climb. These crows are very smart fellows.

Now, some of this, obviously, is tongue-in-cheek, but not all of it.

Those of you who have called our bird question line to tell us about disgusting crow behavior or ask for solutions to problems you have with these highly evolved birds know there is truth to what we say.

Crows belong to the corvid family that includes jays and the magpies. (Oh ho, some of you are saying. Jays and crows are related! Just what you suspected about those disgusting Blue Jays, right?)

Minnesota has five species of corvids–American Crow, Common Raven, Blue Jay, Gray Jay and Black-billed Magpie. Wisconsin has all but the latter. In Minneapolis, St. Paul, Madison and Milwaukee, we contend with only two of those species, the crow and the Blue Jay. You must go farther north to tangle with the other three. North America has four species of crows, all similar in appearance, all intelligent.

Literature is filled with stories about smart crows. Fairy tales include crow characters. Aesop built fables about crows. Today, you can go to the World Wide Web and find a crow homepage.

To say that crows are smart is based on more than observation. Scientists have determined that crows have the largest brains relative to body size of any bird.

These birds are intelligent enough to make and use tools. A biologist, Gavin Hunt, who spent three years studying a species of crow in South Pacific rain forests, reported that he observed the crows making hooked tools. Hunt published his study in the journal *Nature*.

He said that the birds broke twigs from trees, nipping them in an appropriate fashion at their base, then removing leaves and bark. The tool was used to extract insects and other prey from holes in trees. The crow not only used the tool but saved it to be used again.

The list of creatures that make tools is very short. When you want to chase crows from your yard, you are dealing with a worthy opponent. This is a bird that could pick your door locks with a piece of lilac bush and then have lunch in your kitchen!

Once upon a time, crows were exceedingly rare in metropolitan areas. Crows were country birds, pestering farmers, loafing atop those straw-stuffed caricatures staked in fields to scare big black birds away.

But, mankind has lubricated the skids by which crows slid into our midst. Crows are omnivorous; they eat anything. What crow could resist miles of alleys dotted with cans of greasy garbage, the corn put out for deer and ducks, insects in your yard and garden, roadside trash, your birdfeeders and miles and miles of road kill? The city has become a crow delicatessen beyond their wildest dreams. (And don't bet they don't dream!)

Adrienne Krocheski wrote about crows in 1995 for the newsletter of the Wildlife Rehabilitation Clinic at the University of Minnesota. She told of crows known to steal bait and fish from ice fishermen. The birds grasped untended line and pulled, stepping on the slack to keep it from slipping back into the water, repeating this trick until, presto, lunch popped from the hole.

She quoted another author who watched a crow pull the pin from a dog kennel, releasing Fido, then entering the kennel to eat Fido's lunch.

Ms. Krocheski suggested that the city is a safe place for crows. Very few of us here take a gun to these birds when they annoy us. Crows' natural enemies, raccoons and owls, find the city less attractive than the countryside (although there are those of us who would wonder if there could possibly be more raccoons anywhere than in our suburban neighborhoods).

Strong family ties is one reason you see crows in bunches. They mate for life. They are doting parents, sharing responsibilities. And when the youngsters grow up, the adolescents stay at home for a year to help raise the next brood. All the while, the young birds are learning from their elders. Learning about suet and gardens, dumpsters and squashed squirrels.

This skill at acquiring and using knowledge is combined with what can only be described as a sense of fun and play. Crows give every indication of enjoying life. I have no personal observations of crows having fun, but stories abound in the literature. I have seen ravens, however, cavort in the air, playing a game like tag, soaring and diving for no obvious reason.

Best of all, I've seen ravens fly upside down, rolling onto their backs in the midst of straight flight, then righting themselves. I am certain they smile at the same time but I've never been close enough to see that.

A gentleman named Geoff Bell of St. Paul once offered a solution for noisy crows in your yard. He and his mom discovered this and it works, he said. You get a tape or CD containing the calls of hawks and owls. You play these calls loudly from your yard or through an open window when crows are driving you crazy.

"The crows left as soon as we played those calls," Bell said. "And after doing it for several days, they didn't come back."

I believe the crows left. But they left to make a plan. They'll be back and Geoff Bell and his mom had better be ready. — *Jim Williams*

problem birds

How can I keep birds and bats out of my fireplace chimney? I have found them inside the glass doors of our fireplace.

The only certain way to do this is to deny access at the top of the chimney. This is a job for someone who knows what they are doing, since you could affect the way the chimney works or, worse yet, fall off the roof. Call a chimney sweep or other skilled person to screen the top of your chimney.

How can I stop birds from relieving themselves in the birdbath?

You can't. The birds are doing what birds do and you are not going to change that. Birds are beautiful, even if you find some of their habits less so. Relax and enjoy.

Birds keep building nests in my dryer vent. How can I prevent that?

Check your local hardware store for a vent guard that can be installed over the vent pipe as it exits the house. This should deny access to the birds.

My granny used to catch what she called parasite birds, starlings and sparrows. Can we still do that? How about cowbirds?

Yes, European Starlings and House Sparrows, being non-native birds, can be trapped and removed from the environment. Brown-headed Cowbirds, regardless of the problems they cause, are native and thus protected.

Why are some birds (and their nests and eggs) protected and others are not?

Both migratory and non-migratory birds native to North America and not covered by hunting rules and regulations are protected by federal law (in some cases, international treaties). A handful of species that are non-native, that were brought here from elsewhere in the world, are not protected.

About Backyard Birds

How do I find out which species I can't trap or harm?

It is easier to name those species that do not enjoy protection: House Sparrow, European Starling and Rock Dove (common pigeon). Your local office of the U.S. Fish and Wildlife Service can provide more information on this subject.

Can I use discouragement (knocking down nests) on endangered species?

No. Multi-million-dollar construction projects have been brought to standstill by court orders protecting endangered species. Everyone must pay particular concern for the well-being of these species. The U.S. Fish and Wildlife Service keeps a list, as do the various state departments of natural resources. The states also keep lists of those species considered threatened or of special concern.

What are the rules for dismantling nests and destroying eggs and birds?

Nests that are not occupied, not in use or that are under construction can be removed. You cannot remove a nest that has eggs or nestlings. Under no circumstances are you allowed to harm the nest (complete or under construction), eggs, nestlings or adults of endangered species. You cannot keep any nest for any reason. Nests, eggs, nestlings and adults of the three non-native species (European Starlings, House Sparrows and Rock Doves) can be removed.

Where can you buy House Sparrow traps?

Several traps are made for nuisance birds like House Sparrows. One model sold for the past 75 years is available from the Tomahawk Live Trap Co. of Tomahawk, Wis. Call 800-27-A-TRAP. Native species of birds, which are fully protected, might enter the trap. They must be released unharmed. And it does no one any favors if you relocate the birds you have trapped.

Q. I have sparrows picking at the mortar in a brick wall in my backyard. How can I stop them?

A. Perhaps the birds have discovered a weakness in the mortar and are digging a roosting cavity or taking bits of cement as grit. If those little birds can make an impact on that mortar, you have a mortar problem, not a bird problem.

Q. I have sparrows living in my garage. What is the best way to get them out of there?

A. Plug all the holes or possible entries to the building. Keep the garage doors shut. Remove any food attractive to sparrows. We assume you are bothered by House (English) Sparrows. Avoid feeding millet or cracked corn or stale bakery goods. Pull out and destroy any House Sparrow nests you find in your garage or yard.

Q. Do you know of any ways to discourage House Sparrows from coming into our yard?

A. If you want to discourage them from patronizing your feeders, stop feeding whatever they are eating. Don't feed millet, cracked corn, rape seed, bread or stale baked goods. There also is a "magic halo" loop that can be placed over feeders that seems to miraculously deter sparrows. Look for it in wild bird magazines. If you want to discourage them from nesting, remove their nests when found and destroy any eggs you find. When removing bird nests, wear gloves and avoid breathing the dust that might arise. Watch for mice and insects, particularly wasps beneath nest boxes.

Q. While doing some fall cleaning we left our kitchen doors wide open. A chickadee flew into the house. It was a real problem to catch it and get it back outside. How could we have made that job easier?

A. The cardinal rule in dealing with a bird in the house is the same as in *The Hitchhiker's Guide to the Galaxy*: Don't panic. That advice comes from Laura Erickson, bird expert and author. The first thing to do, she says, is make the room the bird is in as dark as possible, closing all drapes and turning off any lights. Perfect darkness makes your job MUCH easier. Locate the bird with a flashlight. Most songbirds will hold totally still as long as you don't shine the light directly at their eyes. If you can't achieve complete darkness where the bird is, try to herd it into a smaller room or a room where you can get total darkness (such as a closet or an interior bath-room). Your eventual goal is to toss a pillowcase or lightweight kitchen towel over the bird. Enclose the bird in fabric and then take it outside and release it. Be gentle. Don't panic.

How can I discourage European Starlings from congregating in my yard?

If they are feeding, change food. Try black oil sunflower seed. If the star-lings are feeding on suet, use feeders that require the birds to hang upside down. Woodpeckers, chickadees and nuthatches can do this. Starlings love suet, but have difficulty hanging upside down to feed. If the starlings are nesting, remove the nesting opportunity. This species is a cavity nester, using holes or nest boxes. Block all possible cavity entrances being used by starlings, but you want to be sure that these cavities are not being used by other species.

How do I keep Purple Finches out of my hanging flower baskets?

These are not Purple Finches, not that the species changes the problem. They're House Finches, a common nester in towns and cities. The males show a bright red-orange color (Purple Finches show more raspberry color). House Finches have a fondness for nesting in flower baskets. You might place screen around the basket or place the basket where the birds have difficulty reaching it or where they are timid to trespass. Or you can just share and relax. You should be able to water the plant even if it shares the pot with a bird family. Don't use so much water that it stands in the planter or soaks the nest. Approach slowly and retreat quickly.

How can I prevent Barn Swallows from nesting under the deck on my house?

It would be best to prevent the birds from gaining access to places where you do not want them to nest. It is more difficult to stop them once they begin building their nests. Hang strips of white cloth close to potential (or chosen) nest sites, from building eaves, for example. Balloons or other objects that move in the wind might be effective. You can remove partially completed nests, hoping to discourage the birds. You might have to do this more than once. You cannot, however, damage or remove the nest or eggs once eggs have been laid. Nor can you harm the birds.

Questions and Answers

Q: Some areas of large cities are plagued with Rock Doves (pigeons). I say plagued because I think they are dirty, messy and not an asset to a neighborhood. What can we do to discourage them from coming into our yard?

A: Not much. Rock Doves are not a protected species; they are not native birds but were introduced here from Europe. That means they can be trapped. Bird traps and/or trapping services are available. Check the Yellow Pages under pest control. Plastic owls also work for a while, but the Rock Doves eventually will learn that the owls aren't a threat. Moving the owl from place to place every two or three days might prolong its effectiveness. You can also use carpentry to exclude the birds from roosting places. And for certain, don't feed millet or bread.

Q: I have pigeons nesting on the corner of the roof on my house. The waste from these birds is clogging my rain gutters. How can I keep the pigeons from nesting here?

A: Pigeons (their real name is Rock Dove) are hard to discourage. They are not protected by law, however, so your options for dealing with them are broad. Try covering the nesting site with half-inch mesh hardware cloth to prevent access. Or, simply make the potential nesting site not level. Pigeons demand a level nest base because they really don't create much of a nest. They more or less lay their eggs on the chosen surface, period. If the eggs roll, that is bad news for pigeons. But it might be good news for you.

Q: I live in an apartment with a balcony. We've got problems with pigeons and small brown birds. The pigeons make a mess on the balcony. The little brown birds make a lot of noise just before sunrise, on cloudy days and in the evenings. How can I discourage these birds from coming to my balcony?

A: If the birds are coming to eat at a feeder, choose another seed. Neither House Sparrows (probably your small culprit) nor your basic city pigeons (which actually are known as Rock Doves) will eat black oil sunflower seeds as readily as they will take other foods such as cracked corn or millet. And neither of those two species is protected by state or federal law, so you can reduce their numbers by humane techniques for trapping and removal. It is hard to discourage sparrows from roosting or nesting anywhere they choose. If you are certain you are dealing with House Sparrows though, you can remove their nests when you find them. House Sparrows are cavity nesters. Look behind boards, under eaves, in tight places. To keep pigeons at a distance, you can also call on the services of the plastic owl. His fierce glare might do the trick.

Is there any way to discourage Killdeer from nesting on my property? I had a problem with these birds last year and now they're back.

Killdeer are tough and brave birds that often don't make the best decisions on nest location (e.g. your driveway or garden path). You might discourage them from nesting simply by being persistent in chasing them away. Remember, please, that these birds, like almost all others you see in and near your yard, are protected by federal law. You cannot harm or kill them. (And most people would be thrilled to have these birds nesting nearby.)

We live on the shore of a suburban lake. Our dock is covered with a tarp. Gulls roost there and they make a terrible mess. How can I get rid of them and keep them away?

Like the skiers say, think snow. The gulls will leave when winter comes and the lake freezes. Short of seasonal change, we can't suggest much. You might try wind socks or decorative objects that flutter in the wind. You could try an owl decoy. But the best anti-gull minds in the country have been unable to shoo them from major airports. Gulls have small but very firm minds.

I have seen a shrike at my feeder. How can get rid of it?

The best thing is to do nothing. Shrikes are a natural part of the entire ecosystem and perform an important function. Shrikes and other natural predators who might keep an eye on your feeders weed out sick and weak birds. The Northern Shrike visits here in the winter. The other North American shrike is the Loggerhead Shrike, an occasional nester in this area. Shrikes are among the birds having a tough time these days. Their numbers are dropping. Be happy if you see one anywhere, even at your feeder. You can offer your feeder birds more protection from shrikes or other predators (like cats, which pose a problem for birds several thousand times greater than any shrike problem) by moving your feeders a bit farther away from bushes or trees so that they have a better view of the surrounding area. This gives them time to escape should a predator threaten.

Questions and Answers

Q: **In the last two weeks, three or four Sharp-shinned Hawks have been cruising my feeders. Several of my neighbors also feed songbirds. Should I be concerned for our songbirds? What should I do?**

A: Do nothing. These predators are a normal part of nature. The loss of a goldfinch or two does not harm the goldfinch population but helps ensure survival of the hawk. Both species belong here.

Q: **Why do we see so many crows around?**

A: Crows, whether you like it or not, and some folks don't, are increasing in numbers. This increase has been steady for the past 100 years or so, for as long as we humans have been exploiting the landscape here. You could say we have brought crows upon ourselves. By changing the landscape and making food available, we have made it possible for crows to spend the winter here, instead of migrating. Also, as those crows which did go south last fall return from their wintering grounds, they are more visible, not yet dispersed throughout their breeding territories.

Q: **What can be done to keep blackbirds and crows away from our feeders?**

A: It depends mostly on what kinds of seed you are putting in the feeders. Try safflower seeds. Blackbirds and crows are less likely to take that. You could also enclose or cover your feeder with 2" x 4" welded wire fencing that will exclude crows.

Q: **I want to attract large birds like Northern Cardinals and Blue Jays. I have a large feeder. I also get crows and blackbirds at this feeder. How to I get rid of the crows and blackbirds?**

A: It is difficult to discourage blackbirds. Feeder placement and choice of food is critical. It will help to keep your feeders distant from coniferous trees. This will discourage grackles and crows, which favor coniferous trees. Use only black oil sunflower and safflower seed. And it is better to have several smaller feeders than one large one.

About Backyard Birds

I have a problem with Common Grackles. They seem to chase other birds away and they foul the birdbath in our yard. I change water three or four times a day and each time the grackles foul it. What can I do about that?

Sometimes there aren't sure-fire answers for keeping birds away from things. It can be hard to attract birds in the first place and then, strangely enough, even more difficult to discourage them. Grackles are native here and very bold in their behavior. Perhaps you could set out more than one birdbath (and hope for the best).

We have four feeders in our suburban yard, with bunches of neat birds throughout the summer. Then, the blackbirds arrived. They have chased the other birds away. What can I do about this?

Those black birds in your yard, most likely Red-winged Blackbirds and Common Grackles, begin forming flocks in August to prepare for migration. It is weather and lack of food which eventually will put them on the road (and they don't go very far, only a few hundred miles south). Expect them to be around until late October or early November. To be rid of them now, keep feed off the ground. Take down your platform or fly-though feeders, perhaps trying tube feeders instead. Black oil sunflower seeds might slow them up a bit. If all of that doesn't work, remove all feed and feeders for a few days, until the birds find a more tolerant host. And since these birds often gather in flocks of thousands, remember, it could be worse.

How can I keep grackles from nesting in the pine trees in our yard? These birds make a real mess and are very noisy.

Grackles will tend to nest high in trees and can be very persistent. We have no good solution for you. By law, you can't shoot the birds and coniferous trees are hard to climb if you wish to place items such as balloons to frighten or distract the grackles. Grackles are among those opportunistic birds which do very well in a city landscape. Sometimes you just have to learn to get along with the annoyance.

Questions and Answers

How can I get rid of the noisy crows that hang around our yard? Last year we had about 20 in our woods.

If squirrels had wings, some folks would call them crows. Both can be very pesky. The crow is a bright bird, perhaps the smartest of all. Our crows have figured out that living in the city/suburbs is a sweet deal. Food is easy to find (they'll eat anything) and predators are few. If you have conifers in your neighborhood, that makes your area even more attractive. Conifers are preferred for roosting and nesting. Also check to see if there is a dumpster nearby, perhaps at a restaurant, that is not crow-proof. A neighbor might be feeding suet and attracting crows. These are problems that can be discussed with those property owners. The easiest thing for you to do would be to build an appreciation for a creature that has proven highly skilled at survival.

birdfeeder problems

How does one keep birdseed from sprouting when it falls from the feeder? If I put it in microwave oven before putting it in feeders will that solve the problem?

Yes. You can nuke sunflower seed, thistle seed and various seed mixes at high power for two minutes per pound. This will kill adult insects, larva, eggs and the ability of the seed to germinate. Put the seed into cotton or paper bags because the plastic bags seeds are sold in will melt in the microwave. You also can treat your seed to 30 minutes in a hot oven, with the same results–insects dead, germination halted. Roast ½" to 1" of seed in the bottom of a 9" x 13" cake pan in an oven at 250 degrees. Give it 15 minutes, then stir and give it 15 minutes more. Do let the seeds cool, however, before offering them to the birds. Will birds know you've cooked their supper? No, they won't have a clue.

You also can buy what seed dealers call parts and hearts, sunflower seeds with the shells removed. This eliminates the hull mess under the feeder, often a problem if you have feeders on a deck or patio. And, because these seeds are usually sectioned, split or cracked, they generally don't sprout.

How can I keep stored birdseed from sprouting and becoming moldy?

Keep it dark, cool and covered. A metal container in your garage would do the job. If you continue to have a problem, buy smaller quantities that you will use quickly.

The seed husks and shells are piling up underneath my birdfeeder. Will this stuff harm the grass when spring comes?

No. You can rake the debris up and carry it away, or use your rake to scatter it, letting nature take its course. An occasional seed might sprout, come spring. Treat those plants like weeds.

What's the best way to cut down on the pile of seeds and shells under feeders? What can I do with that stinky mess in the spring?

You can buy black oil sunflower seed that has been shelled (sometimes called hearts and parts). Many of the birds that commonly come to back yards here will eat that. What falls to the ground will be eaten by squirrels and rodents. The stinky mess you have right now? Rake it up or try your wet/dry vacuum. To prevent such a mess from accumulating next winter, cover the area beneath your feeders with a large tarp. During the warm months, place several patio tiles beneath the feeder so you can more easily sweep up the mess.

I have filled one of my feeders with cracked corn, but every time it rains the corn at the bottom gets wet, then dries into a brick, clogging the feeder. What am I doing wrong?

Cracked corn is best scattered on the ground. Birds that favor this food most often are ground feeders. Better yet, don't use cracked corn. It primarily attracts nuisance species—House Sparrows, European Starlings and Brown-headed Cowbirds.

In winters past, the seed ports on my tube feeders have clogged with snow and ice. Is there any trick to keeping those open?

Placing the feeder in a sheltered spot where it receives less snow and wind might help. Be certain, however, that you don't trade shelter for limited access by the birds. You might just want to continue to go to the feeder after a snowfall and open the feeding ports.

I have a plastic tube feeder in which old seed has turned hard as a brick. I tried to loosen it with Drano, but that didn't work. Any ideas?

Drano? Sounds like overkill. How about a bucket of hot, soapy water and a leisurely overnight soak instead? You might need a narrow tool, such as a long screw driver and some elbow grease for finishing touches. Better yet, recycle the old feeder and treat yourself to a new one. And clean it once a month at least. That's better for both the birds and you.

I feed birds, very successfully. My next door neighbor finds this a problem, saying the birds coming and going from my yard soil her yard and fence. What can I do about this?

Without seeing the yards, it is hard to suggest solutions. You can, to some extent, direct the flight pattern of the birds by the direction in which the front of the feeder (the side from which the birds take feed) faces. Use feeders which dispense feed on one side only and face this away from your neighbor's yard. A large piece of netting strung between the feeders and the fence might be of some help. Perhaps your neighbor has better trees and shrubs for roosting. In that case, plant, plant, plant. And be friendly.

One of my birdfeeding stations is in the middle of a garden area where I grow tomatoes, rhubarb and raspberries. Should I be concerned about the accumulation of bird droppings? Is there a disease hazard?

The bird droppings should not pose any kind of problem unless there is an extraordinary amount. Occasional removal of any accumulation is a good idea, but the natural course of events should accommodate disposal. Of course, you will want to wash any fruit or vegetables.

Birds and Window Glass

When I heard the loud thump against our dining room window a few days ago, I knew a bird had flown into the glass. I had heard the sound before. It is not uncommon when you have birds around your home. If you have bird-feeders in your yard, window strikes become even more frequent.

I went directly to the window to see if I could locate the victim. Sometimes the birds fly into the glass and fly away, unharmed by the incident. Sometimes you see the bird on a nearby branch, recovering but alert. And other times you find the bird on the ground beneath the window, stunned or unconscious.

A clue to the accident, beyond the obvious sound of the impact, painfully loud when you consider how little birds weigh, is the sight of a feather or two pasted to the glass where the bird hit. I could clearly see the mark on our window as I approached. It was large. Several feathers stuck to the glass.

The bird I saw was a medium-sized hawk, a Cooper's Hawk. It was alert and upright, sitting on one of our birdfeeders. It seemed just fine. I watched it for several minutes, trying to determine if it was injured, assuming by the sound of the collision that this bird had been involved. I was correct, this hunter was involved, but not in the way I imagined.

The hawk eventually flew to another perch 20' away. It was then that I noticed the Mourning Dove on the ground beneath the window, its head twisted back over its shoulder, blood coming from a nostril.

The dove had hit the window and died. I assume it was eating at the feeder when the hawk attacked. The dove tried to escape by flying toward the trees and sky reflected in the window. This is the problem with windows.

One spring we found a pair of Scarlet Tanagers dead beside the house. In courtship flight, they had flown one behind the other into unyielding window glass. At our lake cabin, we have had Ruffed Grouse die after such a collision. A grouse hitting your window makes a big noise.

Most of the birds that have struck our windows have lived to fly away. It might take up to 30 minutes for recovery, the bird sometimes panting heavily for several minutes. If the bird is recovering in a warm, sheltered place, in the sun, out of the wind, it seems to do better.

The problem of birds striking windows occurs nationwide. Studies indicate that no less than 100 million birds die each year in this manner. That's one bird for every building in the United States. The actual number might be ten times that large. That's a lot of birds.

Do the windows in your home pose a risk to birds? This is a good question, especially if you feed birds in your yard. To find out, go into your yard and examine your windows at different angles and times of day. If a window reflects the natural environment or pairs with another window elsewhere in the house to create a sight line through the building, consider moving birdfeeders and birdbaths at least 35' away from windows.

There are ways to treat windows to help prevent collisions if you are interested in going an extra step. You can hang objects on string in front of the window. I've used pine cones tied to fish line, stringing half a dozen across the expanse of glass. I tack the top end of the line to the top of the window frame.

A more certain but more complicated preventative is to mount taut, one-inch mesh netting in frames on the outside of the glass to prevent birds from striking the glass. Another option is to put one-inch wide vertical strips of ribbon or tape on the exterior of the glass at intervals of 4" or less. Research shows that few birds will attempt to fly through an opening that small.

Moving your feeders is probably the best solution if you believe you (and the birds in your yard) have a problem. — *Jim Williams*

birds and windows

We have a problem with a robin flying into our windows. It's marking the glass, making noise and soiling the outside sill. We've tried hawk silhouettes on the glass and ribbons hung outside. Nothing works. What can we do?

The bird is seeing its image in the glass and believes the reflection to be a rival. It instinctively wants that other bird to go away. The bird will continue to react through the nesting season. Reduce or eliminate the reflection in the glass. Closing drapes, curtains or blinds on the window might help. Temporarily smear the outside of the window (with an easily removable product) to cut the reflection. Tape a large sheet of paper or cardboard to the window for a day or two. Inexpensive fabric screening from your hardware store temporarily tacked to the outside of the window frame would do the trick. Keep it in place until the bird goes away. That could be several days or even a few weeks.

Birds occasionally fly into our windows and are stunned or injured in the collision. Can I do anything to help them recover?

When a bird flies into a window, it could sustain a potentially fatal injury, but sometimes it is simply stunned for a short time. Unless blood or a black fluid comes from the mouth, it isn't easy to tell how serious a bird's injury is. The best thing you can do for a bird that seems simply stunned is to pick it up off the ground so predators can't get it and put it in a cardboard box in a reasonably warm place (say, a basement). Cover or close the box tightly. NEVER keep a wild bird in a cage even for a short time–the metal bars will fray the wing and tail feathers, compromising its ability to fly when it is released. Line the bottom of the box with paper towels, which are easy for birds to stand on without slipping. Every 10-15 minutes, carry the box outside and open it to see if the bird flies away. DON'T open the box in the house, because if the bird flies in a panic, it may seriously reinjure itself. Open the box slowly, keeping your head out of the way. Do not pick the bird up to help it fly away.

Continue to open the box outside every 10-15 minutes until the bird flies off or you see evidence of a serious injury. In such a case, take the bird to a wildlife rehabilitation center (check your Yellow Pages). If you must keep the bird overnight (no longer than that–it is against federal law to possess a wild American bird), make sure you offer it fluids before dark, let it sleep in the dark and resume your recovery efforts in the morning. Never force-feed any bird food or water; it is best not to feed it at all.

Remember that spring is the season for baby birds to be found out of their nests. These birds probably are not injured. Leave them alone.

The collisions occur because birds see in your window glass a reflection of the outside environment. Seeing sky and trees, they fly into the glass. Some birds glance off the glass and fly away, seemingly no worse for the event. Others can be found beneath the window, stunned, perhaps recovering, perhaps dying.

If your feeder is within 5-10' of a window, it gives the birds sufficient time to reach a flight speed that will injure or kill them if they flush and fly into the glass. Some raptors and crows learn to flush birds from feeders, feeding on birds injured by flying into windows. It is better to put feeders very close to the windows, within a foot or two. This forces the birds to fly away from the glass. Feeders that stick right to the glass also are good, again reducing the possibility of collision. A friend says you can reduce window mortality by sticking a Garfield the Cat doll with suction-cup feet to the outside of the window. Birds won't go near Garfield, he says.

Moving your feeders farther out into the yard also will reduce window strikes. Place the feeders at least 35' from the house in this case.

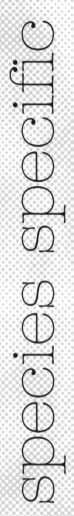

species specific

Eastern Bluebirds

My first experience with trying to lure Eastern Bluebirds to nest boxes was in a backyard in suburban Minneapolis, many years ago. The yard was bounded by a wooden fence. I built proper nest boxes and attached them every 50' or so across the rear of the yard. I then spent the next several summers pulling House Sparrow nests out of the houses and firmly stepping on any sparrow eggs I found.

Let's talk about the sparrows first, since some of you are offended already and I haven't written 100 words yet.

House Sparrows are not native to this area (not even to this continent!) and compete aggressively and too successfully with native birds. Like European Starlings, another introduced species, they are not protected by federal law, as are native birds. This means you can institute your own control program to prevent House Sparrows (and European Starlings) from encroaching on the native species you favor. And I did.

Besides sparrows, I had two other problems with my bluebird program. First, it was unlikely that I was going to find bluebirds in my particular habitat. Second, there were precious few bluebirds to be found anywhere around here 30 years ago.

Today, the situation is different in the most important respect: we have many more Eastern Bluebirds, thanks in large part to the efforts of a dedicated cadre of bluebird fans.

Bluebirds encountered a growing list of problems beginning about 60 years ago. This bird nests in cavities–woodpecker holes, rotted fence posts, such places. We cut down woodlots, cleared land for houses, replaced wooden fence posts with metal. Pesticides were and still are a problem. House Sparrows and European Starlings made life tenuous at best for many bluebirds. The bluebird population crashed.

In 1978, a group of Twin Cities and Minnesota birders, with the support of the Audubon Chapter of Minneapolis, formed the Bluebird Recovery Program (BBRP). This coincided with the formation of a group called the North American Bluebird Society. Both groups are still at work.

The BBRP educated and lobbied and educated some more. It taught people why and how to place nest boxes for bluebirds. It had 3,300 members at one time and over the years sent its large information packet to more than 11,000 persons who wanted to help bring bluebirds back to their neighborhoods.

When the pioneering Minneapolis effort began, there were only two or three other organizations in the country with the same goal. BBRP eventually found members in every state and in Canada. Other state groups were formed to emulate the Minnesota effort.

Today, thanks in large part to the BBRP, you can find nesting bluebirds from the Rocky Mountains east, with exception of far northern reaches.

Can you have bluebirds in your backyard? Yes, if you have appropriate open space. Bluebirds need space, more than an average yard usually provides. You can maintain houses in appropriate habitat elsewhere but you'll need to run a trail, as they say in the bluebird business. You'll need knowledge and some skill to do this successfully, for it takes more than buying a nest box at the hardware store and nailing it to your fence.

Proper knowledge and skills are not hard to find. Thousands and thousands of people from one end of this continent to the other take enormous pleasure in getting to know bluebirds personally. You can join the Bluebird Recovery Program and receive its very informative membership kit by sending a small fee to BBRP, Box 3801, Minneapolis, MN 55403. Also visit the North American Bluebird Society at www.nabluebirdsociety.org. It has links to many wonderful sites. — *Jim Williams*

bluebirds

Can you attract bluebirds in the city?

You are unlikely to find Eastern Bluebirds nesting in the heart of the city. Bluebirds prefer open spaces. Meadows and pastures along fence lines are more likely nesting locations. City golf courses and cemeteries do offer possibilities, however.

How can I attract bluebirds to my backyard?

First, you'll need a backyard with wide open spaces. Small city lots or yards filled with mature trees will not be suitable for Eastern Bluebirds, the species we find here. If you have suitable habitat, pay particular attention to house construction and placement. Check the book *Bluebird Trails: A Guide to Success, 3rd edition* by Dorene Scriven. It tells you everything you need to know about bluebirds and how to attract them to nest boxes.

Sparrows are trying to nest in our bluebird houses. I'm letting them have the one closer to my house but keep cleaning out the second one, which is out in the open, for the bluebirds. Will the bluebirds like this arrangement? I had bluebirds nest three summers ago, but not since then. How can I get them back?

Remove all sparrow nests to improve your chances of success with the bluebirds. There is no peaceful coexistence between these two species. If you had bluebirds nesting once, your chances should be good for a repeat, unless the habitat has changed significantly. Bluebirds need space. Another good reason to remove the sparrow nest is that sparrows sometimes will enter a house occupied by another bird and kill any young found there. It is not hard to recognize a House Sparrow nest. These birds will stuff the house with a surprising assortment of nesting material; they are neither particular nor neat.

Questions and Answers

Q: How high off the ground should I mount bluebird houses? Is three houses enough to attract the birds?

A: Three houses is enough depending on how widely spaced they are. It's a good idea to check your houses frequently for nests of other birds, particularly House Sparrows and Tree Swallows. Bluebird houses or house pairs should be 100 yards apart. Place the houses 5-6' from the ground with the entrance hole facing northeast. Check the box every ten days. Remove the old nest as soon as the young have fledged. Experts suggest you use only the style of house known as the Peterson house.

Hummingbirds
and Orioles

One of the most popular birds seen in anybody's yard is the tiniest nester in this part of the world, the Ruby-throated Hummingbird. This bird can be found nesting throughout the eastern half of the United States. Look for it in deciduous or mixed woodlands, clearings and edges in that land and in gardens and orchards.

There are more than 340 species of hummers in the world, 14 of them breeding in the United States; the Ruby-throated is the only one of those regularly seen in the Midwest. The world's largest hummer is 8½" long, the size of a Northern Cardinal. The smallest hummer–and the world's smallest bird–is the Bee Hummingbird, 2¼" from end to end. Inside those tiny bodies is a heart beating almost 18 times faster than your heart–1,260 beats per minute.

Only about a quarter of all hummingbirds are called by that name. Elsewhere in the world these brilliant little creatures have been given names such as coquette, hermit, mango, wood nymph, sun angel, comet, fairy, mountain gem and woodstar.

Bald Eagles build nests with pieces of wood almost large enough to use for human construction. Hummingbirds use flakes of lichen and strands of spider web to construct their nests. You could cover the top of a hummer's nest with a half dollar.

Hummers are aggressive, readily attacking other birds, the family dog, or you if you are thought to be competing for food or invading their breeding territory. Competition for food is easily observed at any feeder when two hummers arrive at the same time. One of the birds often drives the other off. You can more easily entertain multiple hummers if you post two or more single-port feeders about your yard.

Hummers can easily be attracted to your yard with a bit of sweetened water or appropriate flowers. The birds use long tongues to sip nectar, hovering in front of flowers or feeder ports. While you don't often see them doing so, hummers catch and eat spiders and insects. The protein from small bugs is an important part of the birds' diet. Hummingbirds do not live by nectar alone.

Hummingbirds move through your neighborhood from late April into early June. They begin returning south in early August, peaking about the time school begins. Stragglers can be seen in October.

Just for the record, hummingbirds do not hitch rides at migration time on the backs of larger birds. Our Ruby-throats fatten up and fly across the Gulf of Mexico all by themselves. A good source of information about these birds is the book *Hummingbird Gardens* by Nancy Newfield and Barbara Nielsen.

It you have a hummingbird feeder, put it up in mid-April. The formula for sugar water is four parts water and one part cane sugar, boiled briefly and cooled. You need not color the solution. The birds are attracted by the colored parts on the feeder, not by the solution itself.

This sugar water will spoil in two or three days when the weather is hot. Replace it if it clouds or black fungus appears. Before refilling, clean the feeder well, soaking it for an hour in a solution of two ounces of chlorine bleach in a gallon of water. Rinse well and allow the feeder to dry before you add more nectar solution. You can leave the feeder up well into the fall, until it begins to freeze at night. It will not inhibit migration.

Don't be surprised if Baltimore Orioles and Scarlet Tanagers are attracted to your hummingbird feeders. Orioles like the sugar-water solution, too, taking it when the container is appropriate. You might want to place the solution in a jar with an larger opening for orioles if you see them in your neighborhood. In early summer, when other food sources are not fully available, orioles will take fruit and jelly.

Place your oriole foods on an open platform feeder (flat boards on a post). Be careful about the jelly, keeping it in a container small enough to prevent the bird from standing in the jelly and becoming fouled with it. Bird feathers and jelly do not mix well. A piece of hardware cloth with a ½" mesh, tight to the jelly, makes a good cover for the dish, allowing feeding but not wading. Oranges cut in halves and set on the platform also will attract orioles.

— *Jim Williams*

hummingbirds
and orioles

Where do our Ruby-throated Hummingbirds go in the winter? Do they feed along the way or fatten up here and fly straight through?

Most Ruby-throated Hummingbirds winter in Mexico and Central America, with a few going only as far as Texas or Louisiana. All of these migrants feed along the way to the Gulf Coast, building fat reserves to fuel their flight across the Gulf to their wintering locations.

In October I noticed a very tiny hummingbird, striped with red on its wings, at my flower garden. It was about an 1½" long. What bird was it?

It was probably a White-lined Sphinx Moth, an insect that looks and behaves quite like a hummingbird. They like to feed on flowering plants at dusk. They are most common in late summer. The moths carry under their chins a recoiling proboscis, unrolled to feed in flowers. This characteristic can be used to identify these creatures.

What other species might use a hummingbird feeder?

Baltimore Orioles and Scarlet Tanagers will feed from hummingbird feeders. Some woodpeckers will, too, and Black-capped Chickadees may also give it a try.

What kind of flowers can I plant in my yard to attract hummingbirds?

Try Scarlet Runner Beans, Bee Balm, Cardinal Flower, American Columbine, Coralberry, Evening Primrose, Fuchsia, Gladiolus, Honeysuckle, Butterfly Weed, Morning Glory, Nasturtium, Phlox, Scarlet Sage, Snapdragon, Trumpet Creeper, Bergena, Weigela, Hollyhock, Sweet William and Coral Bells. Planters with Impatiens attract these birds. Baltimore Orioles also will take nectar from some of these plants.

How far above ground should hummingbird feeders be? Should they be in the open or under trees?

Hang the feeder where you can see it and conveniently clean and refill it. This can be from a tree limb or the eaves of your house or a post on your deck. The birds have no preference as to sun or shade, high or low, although placing the feeders out of the sun may prolong the life of the nectar. Squirrels will drink from these feeders, though, so placing them away from the trunks of trees might be best.

When should I put my hummingbird feeder out?

The hummingbirds we see in the upper Midwest, all of them Ruby-throated Hummingbirds, begin their spring arrival here in late April. Migration peaks in late May.

Hummingbirds here are much more likely to nest in areas having significant deciduous or mixed forested areas. They move through the southern half of this area in the spring and fall. Hang a nectar feeder at your lake cabin and you can enjoy hummingbird visits until their early September departure. In the fall, if you keep your feeder fresh and filled into October, November and even December you have a chance of attracting a late migrant.

You even have a chance (very small!) of playing host to a wandering hummingbird migrant of another species. Anna's, Rufous, Magnificent and Calliope hummingbirds sometimes visit here. (Pull out your bird guide book and take a look at those guys, particularly the big Magnificent Hummingbird. It's, well, magnificent.)

One more word about hummingbird feeders: Keep them clean. Each time you refill with sugar water (artificial color is not necessary), thoroughly clean all parts of the feeder to remove the mold that seems to love the nectar as much as the birds do. The mold can be harmful to the hummers.

When should hummingbird feeders be brought in? Will bees and wasps taking nectar from the feeder keep birds away?

Bring the feeders in well after the last hummingbird has departed. This is usually early October but there are November and even December records for hummingbirds in this part of the country. Insects generally will not discourage birds from using these feeders.

How much does a hummingbird weigh?

Ruby-throated Hummingbirds weigh in at just over $\frac{1}{10}$ of an ounce. You could mail about eight of these guys for one first class stamp (if you could get them into the envelope).

Baltimore Orioles come to our nectar feeders in the spring and early summer, then seem to go away. How can I keep them around?

Orioles can be hit and miss. They could be using yard feeders as a source of nourishment until more natural foods are available. Chances are good that your early summer visitors were migrants that nested elsewhere. Keep the feeders clean, changing nectar often. Use feeders with large perches, larger than those for hummingbirds; you can buy special oriole feeders. During nesting season, you could try meal worms. Orioles and Northern Cardinals are among the species that feed caterpillars and larvae to their young. They will come to feeders for meal worms. Ask your wild bird store owner about them.

If we put orange halves out, will orioles come? How do you offer orange halves?

Orange halves will help attract orioles. Secure the fruit on a nail or two placed atop a wooden feeder or a post. Finishing nails, those with narrow heads, work well.

Where should I put jelly for orioles?

A simple, small container like a mason jar lid will work. Put the jelly in the shallow dish and put the dish on a flat wooden platform or post where it can easily be seen by the birds. The smaller the dish, the better. Birds sometimes will stand in a larger dish to eat, their feathers becoming fouled by the jelly.

There is an old Baltimore Oriole nest in a large cottonwood tree in our yard. Will the birds return this spring and use the nest again?

The birds might return to your neighborhood again this year, but they will build a new nest.

Cardinals

Standing in front of his displays of birdfeeders and seed selections, I recently asked a friend who owns a wild bird store, "Which birds are most popular with people who feed birds here?"

"That's easy to answer," he said. "Cardinals are number one by far."

"What's in second place?" I asked.

"Cardinals," he replied.

"Third place?" I asked.

Since I had now figured out the popularity of the crested red birds, we could answer my question together: cardinals!

The Northern Cardinal is one bird that gets along splendidly with man. In fact, if it wasn't for that feeder in your backyard, the cardinals probably wouldn't be this far north at all. The cardinal is the classic story of the guest who came for dinner and would not leave.

How do you get cardinals to your birdfeeding table?

Use the magic bird food. Black oil sunflower seeds (the small seeds, without stripes) are your best bet. Put them in a tray feeder or a tube feeder or just scatter them on the ground where you have swept away the snow.

Keep in mind, however, that cardinals feed early and late in the day. They often appear at feeders in the first faint light of morning, before the coffee is ready, when you might have to look twice to see them. And then they are active again at dusk. This doesn't mean you won't see them in the bright light of noon, but at my house, cardinals and my first cup of coffee are an almost certain combo.

Cardinals also eat fruit, nuts, corn, rice, bread, peanut butter and insects. There are no fussy eaters in the cardinal family. In winter, however, seeds and fruits are 90 percent of their diet.

Cardinals aren't hard to please when you're feeding them and they are equally undemanding when it comes to habitat. They can be found in a variety of habitats–woodlands, farms, small towns and suburban backyards. They favor neighborhoods with thickets and tangled undergrowth, used for roosting and nesting. Honeysuckle is a favorite cardinal nesting plant, as are dense evergreens.

The cardinal moved north from the southeastern part of the country, following settlers and pioneers perhaps 100 years later. Using Minnesota as an example, the first nesting record came from a southern location in that state (Owatonna) in the early 1930s. Today, cardinals are being seen in Duluth and almost as far north as the Canadian border. — *Jim Williams*

cardinals

We recently took a three-week vacation, filling our feeders before we left. The feeders were empty when we returned and now we have few birds and no cardinals. How do we get our cardinals back?

Use black oil sunflower seeds. Keep the feeders full. Scatter some seed on the ground beneath the feeders. Be patient. And next time, hire a young-ster from the neighborhood to regularly fill your feeders.

If I put wooden cardinals in my yard, like decoys, will I be more likely to attract the real thing?

No. If the habitat is not correct for a species, providing the appropriate food, water and nesting opportunities, the birds are very unlikely to be seen there. Decoys will make no difference.

What will attract cardinals to my yard?

Black oil sunflower seeds, thickets and other sources of good, thick cover. Northern Cardinals like evergreens, roosting and nesting in the thickest parts of trees like spruce, cedar and juniper. The Northern Cardinal is a southern bird extending its range to the north. It is common in the southern half of Minnesota, Wisconsin and Michigan. It can be found in the northern portions of those states but is limited to specific locations in those areas.

Will Northern Cardinals nest in a bird house? If not, how can I get them to nest in my yard?

Cardinals are not cavity nesters. They won't use a nest box. Cardinals pre-fer dense thickets for nesting. A big cluster of honeysuckle bushes might be attractive to them, or thick evergreens and cedars. Dense tangles of common garden plants such as roses are good. We're talking serious big and tangled here, unpruned and unkempt, a solid neglected look.

A pair of Northern Cardinals built a nest in a blue spruce tree in our yard, low to the ground. The female was seen on the nest. Then the cardinals were no longer seen near the nest, which contained one egg. Why might they abandon the nest? Is it usual for birds to abandon a nest after they have an egg? House Finches built a nest in the top of the tree. Would this affect the cardinal nest?

There are lots of reasons birds abandon their nests. Perhaps they felt the nest had been discovered and was no longer safe. Perhaps the nest was pilfered by a predator. Perhaps the birds themselves were victims of predation or accident. It is likely, though, that if this pair survived it will try to nest again in another spot. And the House Finch nest is unlikely to influence the cardinals.

We have seen a bird in our yard that looks like a Northern Cardinal but has a black head. What is it?

It is a cardinal with a parasite problem. This is not uncommon and not fatal (unless the bird is infected at very cold times of the year). Feather mites live on the feather bases and weaken them, causing the bird's feathers to break off. There is speculation that dry skin can compound the problem. The black you saw is the natural color of the bird's skin. The parasites will go away. The feathers will grow back. The bird will be—and look—fine.

How many times a year will Northern Cardinals nest?

Many cardinal pairs will produce a second set of eggs in a given nesting season. If and when depends on many factors, including success of the first nesting attempt and weather. If the first set of eggs is taken by predators, renesting is likely to occur immediately. If but one young bird survives to fledgling stage, renesting might occur within two weeks. If more than one young bird fledged, the second set of eggs might be delayed another week. Weather affecting food supply can be a determining factor. Dry weather, limiting food, could cause the cardinal pair to forego a second nest. Birds in northern regions are less likely to nest a second time than birds in areas where the climate is gentle for longer periods of time each year.

Do Northern Cardinals sing more during the breeding season?

Yes, the singing rate of male cardinals and the number of songs per singing session are higher during pre-nesting and nest building periods than during others times of the year. Males sing in courtship display and in territorial defense. Females will sing with males in the period before nesting. There also are song exchanges between mates during incubation and the brooding of young, thought to aid in coordination of male feeding visits to the nest.

Gulls

What do you call those big white birds you see wheeling over the parking lot at the mall?

Wrong. You do not call them seagulls.

A long time ago, I went on a weekend birding tour in Duluth. The guide and teacher for this wet and cold event was a man named Kim Eckert. He was leading us toward a pond when a big white bird came at us through the fog. "Oh, look," said somebody in front of me, "a seagull."

The response from behind me was immediate, loud and definitive. A man said, "There is no such thing as a seagull." The voice of correction came from Bob Janssen, a fine birder and bird book author. He was right, of course. There are no seagulls. So, if the gulls at the mall aren't seagulls, what are they?

They are a large family of birds found worldwide, ubiquitous and successful. Some gulls choose to be near the sea. One species nests high in the Andes mountains. Those we commonly see here favor flatter land and fresher water.

Gulls are undemanding birds. Give them some open water and accessible garbage and you have happy birds. Gulls like malls not for the shoe selections but because we humans generally are a trashy lot. We leave gull banquets in our wake, stray french fries and bagel butts and what-have-you.

Gulls roost on water, generally in different areas than where they feed. When the lakes freeze, the gulls leave. Feeding sites during migration and winter can include landfills, farm fields and large open rivers.

Gulls loaf as well as roost and those activities are different. These birds roost at night and loaf during the day, much as some of us do. Daytime loafing areas are usually separate from nighttime roosts. Loafing areas are usually at or close to feeding sites.

You are most likely to see Ring-billed Gulls and Herring Gulls. There might be a Franklin's Gull in with them, or some Bonaparte's Gulls, both smaller species. Migration produces a handful of other, much more rare gulls.

How do you tell Ring-billed Gulls from Herring Gulls? Since both species have similar plumage colors (white head, breast and belly, gray on the top of the wings and the back, with black on the wing tips) size is a key. You might see both species circling over something in the parking lot that you wouldn't touch with a stick. If you see them together the size difference is quite evident: Ring-billed Gulls are smaller.

Adults of that species also have the namesake ring on their bills, but this feature can be found on immature gulls of other species. The adult Herring Gull has no ring on its bill, just a red spot on the lower mandible (a mandible being one of the two parts, upper and lower, that comprise the bill).

To compound the identification problem, juvenile Herring and Ring-billed Gulls, among others, have an undistinguished dirty look. They show brown colors, darker when they are younger, the brown changing to stronger tones of gray and white as they mature. Many species of gulls take several seasons to reach adulthood, their appearance a bit cleaner and brighter each year along the way.

In the winter, both Herring and Ring-billed Gulls lose their pure white summer head feathers. Winter plumage shows dark streaking on the crown.

If you toss Franklin's and Bonaparte's Gulls into the soup, with their smaller size and black heads, the distinguishing marks to be found in the mix of gray and white on the wings, and, of course, a different winter look, you begin to see why gull identification can be intimidating.

Which explains why some folks just point and say, "Oh, look, a seagull."

— *Jim Williams*

bald eagles

I've seen several Bald Eagles in my life, but I've never heard one call. What do they sound like? Does the eagle have a song?

You might expect the Bald Eagle, a big, strong fellow, national bird and all that, to have a voice like Charlton Heston. Actually, bald eagles sound more like Melanie Griffith. They have a high, thin voice, producing a staccato chirping call almost musical but not a song.

I understand that Bald Eagles migrate along the Mississippi River in the fall. When does this happen and where can we go to see them?

The Bald Eagle migration along the river can be spectacular. Some of the migrants–hundreds of them–will spend the winter where they can find open water on the Mississippi. Beginning about late October and through the winter, check the river downstream from the south end of Lake Pepin in southeastern Minnesota. The city of Wabasha hosts an eagle festival in November. For information, call the Wabasha Chamber of Commerce at 1-800-565-4158.

Early each winter I see Bald Eagles on the ice of lakes in this area. They're often sitting on the ice near open water. Don't eagles go south for the winter?

Bald Eagles go only as far south as they have to, staying one step ahead of the ice as it forms on our lakes. You could see them on local lakes until open water is gone. Much of an eagle's diet is fish. Many Bald Eagles spend the winter along the open water on the Mississippi River. You might see an eagle overhead in the winter, away from water, wandering from place to place looking for food.

loons

In a jungle movie the other night I am certain I heard the call of a Common Loon. Do loons spend the winter in jungle areas?

No. The Common Loon spends its winter along the coasts of North America and in the southern reaches of the Mississippi River. They usually return to the area in which they were reared. Loons will leave their spring/summer lakes in mid-August or September, gathering in larger flocks. These concentrations peak in mid-October. Movie sound editors, however, love the yodel of Common Loons and the scream of Red-tailed Hawks. They insert the calls as background sound, to give the scene some flavor, regardless of authenticity.

Do Common Loons nest in metropolitan areas or do we have to go north to see these birds?

Common Loons may nest on any quiet metro lake with a minimum of human disturbance (especially that caused by personal water craft and motorboats). Common Loons nest across the northern half of Minnesota but are absent in the far western counties. They nest in the northern third of Wisconsin, all of the Upper Peninsula of Michigan and throughout the northern half of the Lower Peninsula. Nonbreeding birds can occasionally be found south of these areas. If you are fortunate enough to have Common Loons nesting on a lake near you, be discrete in your actions and observations. Loons will abandon their nests if disturbed.

If a bird such as a loon dives beneath lake ice, how can it find its way back to the open water?

Loons and other waterfowl that fish for a living have excellent underwater vision and open water viewed from below appears brighter than that covered by ice.

Owls

If you live in the southern half of Minnesota, Wisconsin or Michigan, there is a chance that as many as four species of owl have been in your yard during the past 12 months. You probably have not seen them, but you may have heard one or two.

The four species are Northern Saw-whet Owl, Eastern Screech-Owl, Barred Owl and Great Horned Owl. The first two species are small birds, smaller than an American Robin by a couple of inches.

The Northern Saw-Whet Owl nests in the northern portions of these states, passing through the southern parts of the area from late February through April and again in October and November. It hunts along the way, feeding mostly on small rodents, sometimes small birds and large insects. In the spring, it calls at night as it stops on its journey.

It may hunt at your birdfeeders, taking the mice, shrews and voles attracted by the seed on the ground. It hunts during darkness, so seeing it is a bit of a blessing. Hearing it could be easier. Listen for a tooting note, a repetitive whistle, given at very short intervals, sometimes for hours on end. The bird roosts during the day, preferring conifers, especially cedars.

The Eastern Screech-Owl nests here, hatching young in March or April. This owl uses a natural cavity in a tree for its nest, often employing an abandoned woodpecker hole. It will also use nest boxes. Wood Duck nest boxes often look good to screech-owls.

This bird, too, feeds on small rodents, insects, and sometimes small birds, lizards, crayfish, worms—it is not a fussy eater. It hunts at deep dusk and into the night; it could use your feeder as a meat market. It, too, has a distinctive call, but rarely the screech you might expect. The more frequently heard call has been described as a strongly descending whinny. The bird also has a second song, a whistled single-note trill, often held for seconds, soft as a moth as it floats out of the darkness.

About Backyard Birds

These small owls roost during the day, often tucking themselves beside the trunk of an evergreen tree, deep in its thick foliage. They are not easy to find. Female Eastern Screech-Owls, though, give you an opportunity. They disperse after nesting when the young birds leave. The male owl stays on territory. The female leaves to wander, which is how she might get to your yard. Wood Duck boxes look good at this time of year, too, as places to roost. Check yours in late fall and winter by very gently scratching at its base, then watching to see what sticks its head out of the hole. The birds move about, so it might be here one day, gone the next.

Larger owls offer better viewing opportunities because, well, they're larger. As good a way as any to find an owl in your neighborhood is to listen for the nagging calls of a crowd of crows. Crows harass and chase owls, dogging them with enthusiasm, often attracting Blue Jays and other small birds to join. When you hear crows cry, see what might be at the center of the activity.

Both Great Horned and Barred Owls nest throughout the upper Midwest, the former throughout the area, the latter in the more heavily-wooded portions. Great Horned Owls nest early, on eggs as early as February, sometimes even in January. Barred Owls are perhaps two months behind that schedule. It is possible to distinguish Barred Owls from Great Horned Owls when the birds are perched at a distance or even when they are flying–IF the feather tufts above the eyes, the so-called horns, of the Great Horned species are visible.

Great Horned Owls often take over the stick nest of another large bird, per-haps a nest built by a Red-tailed Hawk. Great Horned Owls often give a firm five-note call–Hoo-hoo; hoo, hoo, hoo. You are more likely to hear it just before dawn, at the end of the bird's work day. In spring, however, some will actively call at dusk.

Barred Owls will use an old stick nest, too, or nest in a tree cavity. Barred Owls have perhaps the most distinctive call. It is translated as, "Who cooks for you, who cooks for you allllll." The Barred Owl is apt to call and call again.

Both of these birds will hunt in your yard or the woods next door. The rodents beneath your feeders (mice get no breaks!) are owl fodder, as are the rabbits in your garden. In the winter particularly, watch for owls perched where they can see your feeders (Barred Owls sometimes perch on the feeder itself). Successful hunters might come back for several days in a row.

Both of these species are more active than the two smaller owls during the time of day when light levels allow observation. Sometimes you can hear the birds calling and follow the sound to the perch. You might even try to mimic the owl call, to draw the bird in as it investigates this newcomer (you), or simply to engage in a bit of conversation. Owls sometimes will answer a skillful rendition. If you are as patient as it is, you might see a large bird sit-ting somewhere, waiting for night and the scritch-scratch of little rodent feet.

— *Jim Williams*

owls

Do owls drink water?

Yes. Owls are no different than other animals in their need for water. Being nocturnal for the most part, their habits and activities are just not obvious to observers.

A neighbor tells us that he has seen a Barn Owl in our St. Paul neighborhood. Is that possible?

It is not likely. Barn Owls are very rare north of the central portions of Iowa, Illinois and Indiana. They are birds mostly of the south and west. Northern states have records of this owl, but only a handful during any 10-year period. There are exceptions. A pair did nest in the early 1990s about 30 minutes south of Minneapolis, using a farm silo to successfully raise four young. Perhaps your neighbor meant to say Barred Owl, a common bird throughout this area. Also, Great Horned Owls sometimes will nest in barns.

Will the owl I hear in our neighborhood attack our pets?

Three species of owls are commonly found in suburban or metro areas: Great Horned Owls, Barred Owls and Eastern Screech-Owls. The first two are larger and they do hunt mammals. A large owl can and will kill rabbits. If your pet is a rabbit, or cat-sized or smaller, then it is possible that an owl could choose it for dinner. But that is very, very unlikely.

Can you feed owls? Can you provide nesting cavities for owls?

You could put live mice or other rodents in an area where you know an owl hunts. This has been done successfully in the winter to assist owls having trouble finding food because of snow conditions. Other times of the year, however, when owls can freely hunt as they choose, it would be much more difficult to place food so the owl would find and take it. A mouse in the summer has much better odds of eluding capture. The answer to the nesting cavity question is yes, Eastern Screech-Owls and Barred Owls will use boxes. The former often can be found in Wood Duck houses.

Q: I want to put up a nest box for Screech-Owls. Where can I buy one, and where should I put it? I have a large maple tree in my yard.

Most of the larger wild bird stores sell Eastern Screech-Owl nesting boxes. You also can find books containing plans. Your bird store should have these as well. Mount the nesting box at least 10' off the ground. It is better to put the box near the edge of a wooded area. Fields or wetlands nearby will help your chances of getting owl occupants. Adding about 2" of wood chips (not sawdust) to the bottom of the box is a good idea. The entrance should be 3" in diameter.

Q: I am hearing an owl calling in my neighborhood, but only after dark. Why do owls call at night and not during the day?

All birds have jobs. Owls are on the night shift. While generally nocturnal, Barred Owls will call during the day, on occasion, and so will Great Horned Owls. That is more likely to happen on cloudy, gray days.

Q: We've had a Barred Owl in our backyard lately. Is there anything we can feed it to bring it back more often?

You can try feeding it live mice. You can buy mice at pet stores which offer them as food for snakes. Release the mouse when the owl is present. A Boreal Owl present at a Minnesota nature center for several weeks one recent winter was fed one mouse each day to supplement the prey it found while hunting. Owls can have trouble finding prey during winters of heavy snow. Don't put out meat such as hamburger; it won't attract owls but it will bring in animals you probably don't want to see.

Q: On my way to the bus stop a few days ago I saw a small owl poke its head out of a hole in a tree in my city neighborhood. What kind of owl could it be?

Most likely, this was an Eastern Screech-Owl. They are common permanent residents throughout the southern halves of states in the Upper Midwest, nesting and roosting in tree cavities, Wood Duck houses and other suitable places. We even know of one screech-owl using a Purple Martin house for roosting. This owl is about the size of a fat robin. It eats rodents and birds throughout the year and insects and an occasional amphibian when they're available.

The other morning, as I was walking to the bus stop, I noticed a flock of crows calling loudly in and around a tree down the block. They seemed to be quite excited about something. What was going on?

Those crows may have been putting the arm to an owl who was just trying to get a good day's sleep. The bird being rousted could have been a hawk, but more likely an owl. If so, it was either the Barred Owl or the Great Horned Owl. The former is the smaller of the two birds, with a round head and no feather tufts (horns) breaking the profile of its face. The Great Horned Owl has those upright tufts, quite obvious if you and the bird are face to face, but hard to see when the bird is in the air. Both of these owls are city and suburban residents. You're more likely to hear them than see them, unless, of course, the crows give you clues. Paying attention to crow gatherings is a good way to locate owls. If your neighborhood crows are carrying on and on, there usually is a reason. Check it out.

We have a big owl in our neighborhood. When I go for walks I try to find its nest, but I haven't seen a nest that looks large enough. What kind of nest does an owl build?

The nest depends on the species of owl. Great Horned Owls use stick nests, often the abandoned nests of crows or hawks. They also nest in tree cavities, which is also the preferred site for the nest of the Barred Owl. As large as an owl nest is, it can be difficult to see, high in a tree and near the trunk. Eastern Screech-Owls, another owl found in urban areas and much smaller than the other two, also uses tree cavities for its nest, often taking an old woodpecker hole. The Great Horned Owl breeding season begins in winter, usually February or March, Barred Owls about a month later. That is a good time to listen for their calls.

Woodpeckers

There are nine species of woodpeckers to be found regularly in Minnesota, Wisconsin and Michigan, the most common among them the Black-and-white House Pounder.

I have chased woodpeckers from my cedar siding and looked with dismay at fist-sized holes chiseled into the side of the house. Doggone pests!

Woodpeckers, however, are solid citizens of the bird world, hard workers, important members of the community, most of them given the unenviable job of working here in the winter, with no beach break.

Our regulars are the Northern Flicker, Yellow-bellied Sapsucker, Downy, Hairy, Red-bellied, Black-backed, Three-toed, Red-headed and Pileated Woodpeckers (house pounder was a joke). Only three members of this family migrate from our region when summer ends, the Flicker, the Red-headed and the Sapsucker. We should note that those three species will winter here on occasion.

Here is a brief look at each species.

Downy Woodpecker. The smallest of all North American woodpeckers, black and white, sexes similar but for red on the mature male's head. Feeds on insects, mostly beetles and ants, but also takes some seeds and berries. Readily takes suet at feeders. Nests in a cavity excavated by both birds in a dead limb or dead tree.

Hairy Woodpecker. A Downy on steroids. A larger black-and-white woodpecker, male also marked with red. The bill is proportionately longer and stouter. It does more excavating for food, less gleaning from the surface of trees and branches, favoring the larvae of wood-boring beetles. Both sexes work to excavate a tree cavity for nesting.

Red-bellied Woodpecker. This handsome bird, showing a fine ladder-like pattern of white marks on its black back, with buff breast and belly, is more common in the southeastern part of the U.S. It has moved into our area in recent decades, expanding its range steadily northward. It, too, takes insects, but may find half of its nourishment from plant material at some times. The male begins excavation of several holes in a tree, pole, post or stump; the female chooses the location to be finished for the nest. The red on the belly is a bit of blush during breeding season, almost impossible for an observer to see. The red slash covering its head from eyes to nape is hard to miss (unless you are naming the bird).

Red-headed Woodpecker. This bird, well-named and hard not to recognize, is slowly fading from our landscape. It was much more common years ago. It favors areas with large scattered trees, groves and orchards. There are many reasons for the reduction in population, perhaps chief among them habitat change. Red-heads eat many things, including insects, nuts, berries, earthworms, fruit, sometimes eggs and nestlings of other birds, tree bark, and, rarely, small rodents. These birds excavate a nesting cavity in a bare dead tree or dead limb.

Yellow-bellied Sapsucker. You have to love this bird for its name alone. It is midway between the Downy and the Hairy in size, with a yellowish belly, red atop the head and a red throat on the male. Juveniles look like faded versions of adults, not colorfast. There are four sapsuckers in North America; this is the only one regularly present in the upper Midwest. It does eat sap, drilling a sometimes very neat line of small holes in trees, from which sap oozes. The bird returns to its work to eat sap which comprises about 20 percent of its diet that includes insects and fruit. Both sexes work to excavate the nest hole, often in trees affected by a fungus that makes the heartwood soft. Experts can distinguish between the rapping patterns of woodpeckers. You can pick sapsuckers from the crowd. Listen for a rap that begins rapidly, then slows to spaced single raps.

Northern Flicker. This is our second largest woodpecker, a good foot in length, brownish overall, marked with smart barring on its back and stylish spots on its breast and belly. It shows a wide black slash at the throat. Look for bright color beneath its wings (usually yellow, rarely red) when it flies. Flickers are often seen feeding on the ground. This is because they eat more ants than perhaps any other North American species. They take other insects as well, along with fruits and berries, seeds and nuts. Both sexes work to dig the nesting cavity, most often in dead wood.

(The yellow and red variance in underwing color once helped describe two separate flicker species that since have been combined into a single species, the Northern Flicker. The red form is rare east of the Dakotas. The Gilded Flicker, found in the far west, is a separate species.)

Pileated Woodpecker. This is the Big Guy, over 16" long, with a 30" wingspan. It is black with a white stripe running off its face down the side of the neck. Both sexes have red crests; the male adds a slash of red on its face, touching the bill. These birds are found throughout the Great Plains east with the exception of the far west and southwest. They feed on ants (mostly carpenter ants), termites, larvae of wood-boring insects, other insects, fruits and nuts. They excavate a large cavity for nesting, perhaps 18" deep. It may take the birds three to six weeks to finish the nest site.

Black-backed Woodpecker and Three-toed Woodpecker. Both of these uncommon boreal-forest birds are about the size of a Hairy Woodpecker. Both are specialists in beetles and larvae that damage trees. Both favor burned areas, where dead and dying trees can be found. Both excavate cavities in trees for nesting, the Three-toed making a new cavity each year, something the other species do not always do.

Other than woodpeckers, there are 27 species of birds nesting in the Midwest that use tree cavities as nest sites, including chickadees, nuthatches, flycatchers and swallows. Some mammals use the cavities woodpeckers create. That means the excavation work done by woodpeckers is of major importance to the survival of other birds and mammals, because none of those species is equipped to dig a hole in a tree.

Man has a role here also, given our inclination to remove dead and dying trees from the landscape. Dying trees attract the insects on which woodpeckers depend for much of their food. Dying and dead trees and dead snags in otherwise healthy trees are the raw material for homes for these creatures. The chain extends from us to trees to woodpeckers to other birds and animals. We all are connected.

Woodpeckers get another star beside their name because most of them are full-time residents here, spending their winter months scouring trees for over-wintering insects and insect eggs. They serve as major factors in forest insect control.

And now, the ultimate question: Why do woodpeckers drum? Because they can't play guitar. Also, to announce their presence, establish territory, keep mating rivals away and attract a mate. Why do they drum on your house? Because the bird senses insects beneath that siding or in the cracks, because your house gives off a loud and potent sound when rapped, or perhaps because the natural drumming sites in your neighborhood have been removed.

One way or another, the drumming carries a message. — *Jim Williams*

woodpeckers

Woodpeckers are drumming on our house. They are making both noise (very early in the day!) and holes. What can we do to stop them?

The birds might be looking for food or simply using your house as an amplifier for territorial drumming. Spring is the time of year when woodpeckers are seeking mates and establishing turf. If the area under attack is small, it can be covered with heavy plastic material, a tarp or even fine-mesh window screen to prevent access to the area and break the habit. If the birds are looking for food, they are telling you that insect infestation is the core of the problem. There are bugs or eggs in the cracks and crevices of the siding. Insecticides are not useful and can be harmful to both you and the birds. Ask a paint retailer about products that protect against insects. Children's pinwheels or aluminum pie pans hanging so they blow with the breeze and make noise also will frighten birds away from an area. If holes or cavities begin to appear, they should be filled promptly with caulking or wadded fine screen mesh to discourage the birds; they might be thinking of a nest and really get serious about a hole.

Woodpeckers working on your house could be bored youngsters. We recently read of a Canadian researcher who found that woodpeckers digging holes in her house were for the most part young birds prevented by their elders from eating at nearby feeders. They whiled away the idle time by working on her house, she said. Eventually, digging on the house became a habit. The researcher learned to control this by not feeding woodpeckers from mid-May to early August, when juveniles were present.

A house owner troubled by woodpeckers solved her problem with menthol/eucalyptus ointment, the kind mom used to rub on your chest when you were a kid with a cold. She said she smeared the ointment on the house where the woodpecker was pounding. It came back one time, she said, then never was seen again. (And its cough went away, too.)

Mylar balloons attached at the point of attack and plastic owls posted as sentinels also have been reported to work. The trick with the owls is to turn them every so often so they don't appear so plastic.

Do woodpeckers sing like other birds?

Not really. Some species of woodpecker have a chatter-like call, others just a sharp note or two. The calls are different for each species and with practice you can learn to tell one from another.

Do woodpeckers use their nesting holes for shelter and sleeping during the non-nesting part of the year?

Occasionally, they do this. Woodpeckers, chickadees and nuthatches, the species that winter with us, often will seek shelter in woodpecker holes or other cavities to escape harsh weather.

I have two black and white woodpeckers coming to my suet feeder. One is much larger than the other. Are these male and female, a pair?

No. They are most likely a Downy Woodpecker, the smaller bird, and a Hairy Woodpecker, the larger. These are the most common woodpeckers in this area. To identify these birds when they are not together, when size gives you all the clue you need, look at their bills. The Downy Woodpecker has a small bill, almost like a songbird. The bill of the Hairy Woodpecker is long and stout. Also, the Hairy Woodpecker has a larger arc of black on its shoulder, a hook of color that curves into the white sides of its breast. Males of both species have red at the back of the head; females lack this red mark.

We see Pileated Woodpeckers in our neighborhood. What can we offer as food to bring them to our yard?

Suet. Use large unprocessed chunks in a big feeder firmly attached to the top of a platform (hardware-cloth baskets and ½" mesh work well to hold suet; avoid suspended feeders that sway or wiggle). Place the feeder away from the house; Pileated Woodpeckers are more cautious than Downy or Hairy Woodpeckers.

If the Northern Flicker is a woodpecker, and my bird book says it is, why don't I ever see flickers pecking at trees like other woodpeckers? I usually see flickers on the ground, like robins.

The bird world is filled with specialists. The Northern Flicker has adapted to finding much of its food on the ground. It is particularly fond of ants, but will eat other insects. It does behave in typical woodpecker fashion in other respects, among them creation of a tree cavity for nesting.

We have something drilling holes in a perfectly straight line in the cedar siding of our house. Is this a woodpecker or some other pest?

Woodpeckers usually don't drill holes in a straight line. The Yellow-bellied Sapsucker, a species of woodpecker found here, will make such holes, but this bird does it to draw sap which attracts insects the bird eats. Your cedar siding is not giving up sap, but cedar paneling has horizontal gaps between the inner layers of paneling. Insect larvae can enter these gaps from the sides of the paneling. Woodpeckers will hunt along these larvae-filled cavities.

Do all woodpeckers have red markings?

No. Red on the head of several species of woodpecker indicates a male bird, but we have two species here, the Black-backed Woodpecker and the Three-toed Woodpecker, for which neither sex shows red. These are the only woodpecker species in North America in which the male lacks any red markings.

sightings and questions

Identifying Birds

Birdwatching has its embarrassing moments.

If you play golf, maybe you've stood on the first tee, with other golfers casually gathered behind the ball washer, waiting for you to clear the tee box. You step up to the ball, waggle the club head and cleanly miss the ball on the downswing. A complete red-faced swish.

The corresponding moment for birders is to see a bird, point it out to a crowd of people and then in a firm, strong voice misidentify it.

"Osprey!" you call loudly, as you see the bird for a brief moment before it wheels out of sight behind some trees. When it reappears in a few seconds it has somehow changed to an immature Bald Eagle.

Oops.

It's not easy to cleanly hit golf balls. Nor is it easy to identify every bird you see. Practice helps in both cases and there definitely is a method to the madness of telling one bird from another when you are trying to match a snatch of memory with those pictures in the field guide.

Someone recently called the Minnesota Ornithologists' Union to report a sighting of a Mountain Bluebird. This is a western species rarely seen east of the Missouri River. The male is sky blue, darker on the head, back, wings and tail, lighter on the breast and belly. The caller left a perfect description of a Tree Swallow. Tree Swallows are deep greenish blue on the head and back, with some brown mixed into the wings and tail; the breast and belly are white.

How do you confuse two such different birds? How do you confuse an eagle with an Osprey?

It's easy. Every birder has done it at one time or another.

Many people look at a bird, form a general picture of it in their mind, then begin paging through the field guide, looking for a match.

"Aha," they say, finger on the page that presents the first possible match. "Here it is. It looked just like this."

Except the bird beneath the finger isn't supposed to be this far east of the Rockies. Or it is half the size of the bird seen. Or twice the size. Or has wings of a different shape. You get the idea.

If you want to sharpen your identification skills, consider these points.

Look at the entire bird. Make notes (on paper if you can, in your head if you must) about its size, shape, color patterns, obvious marks and behavior.

Is it the size of a chickadee, a blackbird, a robin, a crow? Larger than one of those? Smaller? Using common birds as size guides can help you significantly narrow your choices for identification.

Does the bird look long and thin? Short and stubby, maybe? What shape is the bill? Finches, for instance, have short thick bills, the better for cracking the seeds they eat. Warblers have much thinner bills, adapted for plucking insect larvae from leaves and branches. Once you get to the book, knowing that the bird is not a finch or not a warbler, for instance, makes your ID task easier.

What color is the bird and how are the colors distributed? Look at the head and face, at the folded wings (if the bird is not flying) and the tail. Are there obvious facial markings? Bars on the wings? How many? Markings on the tail, bands perhaps? Thick bands or thin?

What is the bird doing? Is it on the ground or high in a tree? Sparrows, for instance, are ground birds for the most part; many of the warblers prefer more height to their activities. How does the bird fly? Some soar, some flap continually. Woodpeckers fly in a scalloped pattern, their flight path resembling a child's drawing of waves on an ocean.

Where was the bird seen? On a lakeshore, in a meadow, in the woods? Some look-alike birds are found in very different habitats and birds tend to be where they are supposed to be. Habitat often is the critical factor in an identification decision.

With all of the information you have gathered by really LOOKING at the bird, take your notes (mental or otherwise) and open the identification book. You want to match your notes with the information in the book. Your identification will be made easier if you know more than just the color of the feathers.

(Yes, sometimes all you know for certain is the color of the feathers.)

Remember that many birds share colors. For example, not all blue birds are *bluebirds*. Some blue birds are swallows or buntings or grosbeaks or even jays. Some blue birds are common here and others are not. It is possible in the upper Midwest to see Indigo Buntings, an all-blue bird but not a *bluebird*. Check the size of the bird. Compare the patterns of blue. Look for other colors. Look at the bills. Be patient and be careful. Don't jump to conclusions.

Ospreys and eagles? An adult Osprey has white on its head and a dark upper body and tail, as does a Bald Eagle in its third or fourth year (Bald Eagles take five years to achieve complete adult plumage). But Ospreys have longer, narrower wings with an obvious crook to them as you watch the bird fly. Eagles soar with flat wings that often show what look like fingers at the ends, as the primary feathers separate on the beat.

Does this sound impossible? It isn't. Take time to look at the entire bird. Get to know that individual. Apply your observation carefully to the guide book. And practice, practice, practice. You recognize friends on the street because you know them. The same thing applies to birds.

One last note: You won't be able to identify them all. None of us can.

— *Jim Williams*

what bird is that?

Q: The starlings that were coming to my feeder this winter seem to have been replaced by different birds this spring. The new ones are shaped like starlings but are colored differently. What are they?

A: They're starlings in a different plumage. European Starlings are among the birds that change coloration with their seasonal molts. In spring and summer, starlings have an iridescent shine to their plumage and a yellow bill. In winter, the birds are heavily speckled and the bill is dark. The speckled tips of the feathers wear off as the winter progresses.

Q: Why does the black throat patch of the House Sparrow seem to be more visible in late winter?

A: Your clothes wear out. Birds have the same problem. By late winter the buff-colored tips of the black feathers on the sparrow's throat patch get worn away. Some other birds also change appearance somewhat during the course of the year because light-colored feather edges become worn. Red-winged Blackbirds show bright yellow on their shoulder patch in early summer, when the birds have fresh feathers. This yellow becomes less visible as the year progresses and feather wear becomes evident.

Q: Now that it's spring, birds are beginning to return to our neighborhoods. Do you have any recommendations for people who would like to know the names of all the birds they see and hear?

A: Take a field guide, a pair of binoculars and go outside. Begin with the common birds in your yard or neighborhood and have patience. Don't expect to correctly identify every bird you see. Even experts can't do that. Begin by assuming that the bird you see belongs here; don't try to make it an exotic visitor from afar. In addition to checking the pictures in your field guide, read the text and use the range maps. Look at more than just the color of the bird. Behavior is often just as important. Remember that males and females of the same species often look quite different from one another. Work on one bird at a time. It is helpful to begin with the birds you see most often. When you can identify the common birds by sight and call, it is easier to recognize those that are new or uncommon.

Is there any trick to bird identification?

Each family of birds has a different set of jobs. Some work in the air, like swallows or swifts. Some work in treetops, like certain warblers. Some work in bushes, like Gray Catbirds or Brown Thrashers. Some work on lawns, like American Robins. Other birds like tall grass in open fields (meadowlarks) or the marshy shore of a lake (herons). Learning the habitat preferences of the various families can make identification of the individuals within the families much easier. Read your field guides for this information and use your own observations.

How do I keep from frightening the birds I want to see up close?

Be quiet. Move slowly and smoothly. Noises and quick motions will drive birds away. Hold back if you begin to disturb the bird. Remember, the well-being of the bird always comes first. Outdoors, you are a guest in the bird's home; act accordingly. If you are good to the bird, chances are the bird will be good to you.

In mid-December in the vacant lot next door we saw a gray bird with a black mask. It perched at the very top of a small tree. What was it?

It sounds like you saw a Northern Shrike. These small predators (catbird size) come here in winter from breeding locations far to the north. Some years they are more conspicuous than others. The shrike feeds on small birds and rodents during its time here. It often impales its prey on thorns or another sharp object like barbed wire, then eats. The bird's feet are not strong enough to hold all prey firmly while eating. Sometimes, the shrike leaves impaled prey as a cache, returning later to eat.

Not all of the juncos feeding in our yard look alike. Is there more than one kind of junco?

There are several subspecies (or races) of juncos. Some are more common than others, depending on where in North America you live. The common race here is the Slate-colored Junco. The Oregon Junco is also occasionally seen here while the Gray-headed Junco is seen here very rarely.

Questions and Answers

How can I tell one species of sparrow from another?

The same way you get to Carnegie Hall—practice, practice, practice. First, look at your calendar. Certain species of sparrows can be expected at certain times of the year. The turn of the New Year would be a good time to begin because winter sparrows are few in number. Get out your field guide. Turn to House Sparrow, that scruffy little pest from Europe. Study both male and female. Now turn to American Tree Sparrow, a handsome bird with a small spot centered on its breast, like a stickpin. Learn these two species. Knowing the common species and where and when they are found will make it easier for you to recognize the less common birds. Beginning in late March or early April we will have Fox Sparrows, Song Sparrows, White-crowned and White-throated Sparrows, Chipping Sparrows and several more. All are unique. All can be identified with practice and patience.

Just before Christmas I saw hundreds of black and white ducks on a large lake near my home. They were in open water far from shore. What species of duck would stay here so late?

Several species of waterfowl will linger until lakes freeze, including Common Mergansers, Buffleheads and Common Goldeneyes, all of which are black and white.

What kind of birds call at night? We've got one in the field behind our house calling all night long.

Many birds call at night. Among those you might be hearing are owls, Whip-poor-wills, Common Nighthawks, Mourning Doves, American Robins, rails, the American Woodcock and certain sparrows, wrens and blackbirds. Perhaps listening to a recording of bird songs would provide your answer. Don't eliminate the possibility of frogs and toads. On late summer nights there also is an insect called the Snowy Tree Cricket that is incredibly loud and often mistaken for a bird.

I have a bird in my yard that says "Yoo-hoo." What is it?

Black-capped Chickadees have a call that could be characterized as yoo-hoo. This particular chickadee call is two notes, the first higher than the other.

Q: I have a new bird at my feeder. It is small and slender with brown stripes on the breast and yellow marks on the wings. What is it?

A: It sounds like you are seeing Pine Siskins. These birds, which behave much like the more common American Goldfinch, nest in many locations here and are erratic winter visitors. Some winters you might see a handful. Other winters they come to your feeders by the dozens. They eat seeds and will feed at your hanging feeders or on the ground.

Q: This summer I planted sunflowers in my backyard. Now I'm seeing a bird I've never seen before. It's the size of a sparrow, colored yellow with black on the wings. It feeds on the seeds in the dried flower. What is it?

A: You are entertaining American Goldfinches. A favorite feeder food for them is sunflower seed and they'll take it from the source as well as from the feeder. Sunflower plants are a good crop for people who feed birds. Just let the plants stand in the garden. The birds will find them. You can also buy the dried flower heads with the seeds intact and hang them in your yard for finches and other seed-eaters.

Q: Why do all the sparrows in my yard have red on them?

A: Because they're House Finches. A House Finch is about the same size as a House Sparrow. It is colored with red or red-orange and is becoming more and more common.

Q: For the last three weeks, I've heard a bird or some animal call at 1 a.m. every morning. It's a screeching sound, one short call followed by a long one (that curves upward in middle). This is repeated from six to ten times, loudly. Any idea what this could be?

A: It could be an owl or a raccoon or your neighbor's cat. The latter sounds most likely, given the punctuality of the cries. Birds and wild mammals are hardly so punctual, but your neighbor might be letting his tabby out every night at the same time. If you hear this in late summer, it could be the insect known as the Snowy Tree Cricket.

Questions and Answers

The European Starlings around my house don't seem to have a song like other birds, instead making a variety of noises. Am I hearing this correctly?

Yes. European Starlings, the birds you are hearing, are mimics. They make a wide variety of noises, squeaks, whistles and calls.

Earlier this fall there were a lot of different birds feeding on bugs in the air in our neighborhood, a variety of swallows, martins and blue-birds. How can you tell one species from another when they are flying?

Choose one bird. Study it closely. Does it flap and glide? Does it soar? How large is it? Note the color and pattern on its head, belly and wings, the shape of its tail. Is it feeding over land or water? Take this information to a field guide. Learn that bird. For birds in general, learn to identify the common species, then move on. Knowing a few birds well makes it easier to spot and eventually identify others.

We had a Black-headed Grosbeak at our feeder in August. How unusual was that?

It would be most unusual. It is much more likely that you saw an immature male Rose-breasted Grosbeak or perhaps an Eastern Towhee. These birds would be common here at that time of year. The female and immature Rose-breasted closely resembles the female Black-headed Grosbeak and the towhee is sometimes mistaken for a male Black-headed Grosbeak. Because of the time of year, we suspect the bird you saw was a young Rose-breasted Grosbeak. The problem is, not all guidebooks show immature birds.

We had an olive green bird with black wings, about the size of a Rose-breasted Grosbeak at our feeder. What was it?

Turn to Scarlet Tanager in your bird book. Check the female of that species.

From a window on an upper floor of the IDS Tower I watched a large bird kill a pigeon. What was the predator?

It was most likely a Peregrine Falcon. Peregrines have been the subject of an intense reintroduction program over the last 15 years. The effort has been hugely successful throughout the Midwest. Breeding season begins in March.

We live on a marsh. Occasionally, we see a very small waterbird with a very short bill. It usually dives and disappears as we approach. What is it?

It sounds like you are seeing a Pied-billed Grebe. This is the smallest member of the grebe family to be found here. It is a shy bird rarely seen on the wing, preferring to avoid you by diving and swimming away underwater, as you describe.

In the city, I occasionally see small birds without tails flying fast over the buildings. What are they?

They are Chimney Swifts and they have tails, albeit stubby tails. Swifts are swallow-like but of a different family. They are aptly named, often nesting in chimneys. They will also nest in open well shafts, open silos and tree cavities. They build a half-cup nest of twigs glued together to the wall with their own saliva.

I watched a very small bird, perhaps a warbler of some kind, feeding a huge baby. The young bird was about four times the size of the parent. Why was that?

The parent bird undoubtedly was feeding a Brown-headed Cowbird. Cowbirds are members of the blackbird family. They are nest parasites, laying their eggs in the nests of other birds. The host bird often, but not always, raises the cowbird to maturity, usually at the expense of some or all of its own young. Cowbirds grow to be about the size of Red-winged Blackbirds. They demand much food from the often smaller host parent.

Questions and Answers

How can I tell the difference between blackbirds, crows and ravens?

Common Ravens and American Crows are closely related. They are large, completely black birds. Crows, the smaller of the two species, are common everywhere in the Midwest. Ravens, however, are found only in the boreal regions of the northern counties and rarely associate with people. Ravens give a metallic croaking call, very unlike the common "caw" note of the crow. Blackbirds are very different in many ways from crows and ravens, no more closely related to those species than are robins or goldfinches. Some blackbirds (in this area family members are Common Grackle, Rusty, Brewer's, Yellow-headed and Red-winged Blackbirds and Brown-headed Cowbird) aren't even all black, often marked with iridescence or a bright splash of color.

I have a bird in my yard that looks like a sandpiper. Is it a Killdeer? Where do they build their nests?

It probably is a Killdeer, an abundant bird throughout the central United States, both city and country. These birds nest on the ground, in a spot of sand or gravel or in the middle of your driveway. They often choose nest sites inconvenient to the landowner. Be alert.

I have a pair of small, gray, long-tailed birds nesting in my yard. Their call is a thin whistle. What are they?

It sounds like you are hosting Blue-gray Gnatcatchers. These active birds are small and slender, like chickadees on a diet. They build a deep, rounded cup nest in trees or shrubs. Gnatcatchers are birds of the south and east that have gradually moved to more northern climes, like Minnesota and northern Wisconsin and Michigan. Seventy years ago they were rarely seen this far north.

We are supposed to have both Western and Eastern Meadowlarks in the neighborhood of our hobby farm in south central Minnesota. How can I identify each species?

The two species look alike. It is the song that will tell you which bird you have. Eastern Meadowlarks usually sing a clear, four-note song. Westerns produce a few distinct notes followed by a confusing warble.

Q: We have observed a flock of 15 to 20 Cedar Waxwings in our suburban neighborhood several times this winter. Are these birds common at this time of year?

A: Cedar Waxwings spend the year here, almost always traveling in flocks, oftentimes larger than those you have seen. This species feeds on fruit and insects. Watch for them in juniper and wild cherry trees.

Q: This fall I thought I saw a juvenile Red-headed Woodpecker in my yard. Was that possible?

A: Yes, especially at that time of year when juvenile birds would be present. Red-headed Woodpeckers, unlike most other Midwest woodpeckers, prefer open space away from large expanses of dense woods. They often are seen in wooded pastures or on power poles along roads in states from the Rocky Mountains east. This is a species in decline because of both summer and winter habitat loss.

Q: This fall, in a park near our home, we saw small flocks of Yellow-rumped Warblers and kinglets. It was really exciting. Does this mean we will see birds here during spring migration as well?

A: Actually, spring migration in your neighborhood—in any neighborhood—should be even better than fall. Spring migration is condensed, the bird population moving through in a shorter period of time, driven by the urge to reach nesting territories. Fall migration is protracted, birds often stopping to feed and rest until driven on by a change in the weather.

Q: There was a large black bird in my yard recently. It looked too big for a crow. Is it possible it was a raven?

A: If you live more than 150 miles from the Canadian border, that is unlikely, but it is possible. Other than size, the obvious differences to look for when distinguishing between American Crows and Common Ravens are the larger bill in the latter, its much longer wedge-shaped tail and a larger-looking head. Ravens also show a "shaggy" beard of feathers at the neck.

Q: Are there game birds like pheasant and grouse in metropolitan areas?

A: Ring-necked Pheasants can be found in many suburban communities. They will readily come to ground-feeding stations offering cracked or whole corn. Gray Partridge can also be found in certain areas. Wild Turkeys occasionally are seen and these are legitimate wild birds. Birdwatchers sometimes report Northern Bobwhite, Chukar and other non-area birds in their neighborhoods, but these surely are captive birds that have flown the coop. Bobwhite, for example, are rare north of a line through Iowa's northern border. And Chukar are non-migratory birds found in the far west.

Q: I had a Brown Thrasher at my feeder daily during the month of March. A friend says that could not be. What do you say?

A: Tell your friend that Brown Thrashers sometimes spend the winter in their summer territories, all the way to the Canadian border.

Q: There is an all-white sparrow at my feeder. What is it?

A: Full or partial albinism is quite uncommon in House Sparrows but it does occur. If the bird otherwise appears, acts like and flocks with House Sparrows, it probably is one. If not, it may be necessary to observe all the details you can about its size, shape, feeding habits and behavior. There are usually enough other observable markings to figure out what it is, but not always. It should survive just fine, like any other of its species.

Q: I work near the Mississippi River. Sometimes, I see large dark birds flying over the river area with wings held in a slight V. They have feather fingers on the end of their wings. Can they be Turkey Vultures?

A: In all likelihood, the birds you have seen are Turkey Vultures. They are regularly seen to the Canadian border and nest throughout the area. They can be identified by the feather fingers at the end of their wings and by the way they hold their wings slightly above horizontal in the shape of a very broad V when gliding. Bald Eagles—the juveniles are large and dark—glide with their wings held almost perfectly horizontal, without the V-shape.

About Backyard Birds

We've seen Trumpeter Swans on a drainage pond near Minneapolis. Is this unusual?

Until recently, it would have been most unusual. Trumpeter Swans, once native to the upper Midwest, were extirpated in the 1800s. About 30 years ago, a reintroduction program began, a most successful effort. These swans, largest of North American waterfowl, are doing well in various Minnesota and Wisconsin locations and can occasionally be seen at small ponds and marshes throughout the area.

Do we have Scarlet Tanagers in metropolitan areas?

Yes, but they have very specific habitat needs. You are most likely to find them in large, unbroken areas of mature forest. Check with the county park or nature center nearest your home.

Does the American White Pelican nest in Minnesota?

There are a few sites in the state where they nest, including places in Lake of the Woods and Lac Qui Parle counties. Nests recently were found on Minnesota Lake in Faribault County and Lake Johanna in Pope County. During the summer, these birds wander widely and can be found just about anywhere they can find food. American White Pelicans occasionally even stay here for the winter, if there is suitable open water.

Bird Longevity

How long do birds live?

On average, not long. They have potential for longer lives, but it is rarely realized.

We have a local story of a Common Grackle which made it to the very old age (for a small wild bird) of more than 19 years. Part of the problem with answering the question of bird age is that birds don't have birth certificates or apply for driver's licenses; it is very difficult to keep track of an individual bird.

The grackle, however, had been banded early in its life. Its band, like all official bird bands, was coded with the date the band was applied. Thus, if recovered, the band would yield an age.

The grackle's banded leg was found in the nest of a pair of Peregrine Falcons. The rest of the grackle apparently had been fed to the falcon chicks. Before meeting the peregrine, the grackle had been old enough to vote.

A recent report on Whooping Cranes preparing to leave their Canadian nesting territories to return south (mostly to Texas) for the winter provides a lesson in bird mortality. The cranes, so few in number, are closely monitored. Aerial searches for newly hatched birds were conducted in early June with 47 chicks sighted. Less than three weeks later another check found only 32 youngsters. What happened? The report simply referred to "the usual mortality of very young chicks."

That phrase could be applied to the cardinals and chickadees nesting in your yard. If the neighbor's cat didn't get them, the raccoons did. If the cowbird that hatched in the warbler nest didn't crowd the warbler babies onto the ground or simply command all the food brought to the nest, bad weather did the job.

Bird life, especially that of young birds, is filled with threat and danger.

Under ideal circumstances–adequate food, appropriate weather, no predators–birds can rival humans in life spans. The Guinness Book of World Records in 1980 listed a parrot supposedly 104 years old. A condor lived 72 years in a zoo. Captive hawks, eagles, pelicans, owls and ravens have made it to the half-century mark. A captive Northern Cardinal has been reported to have reached its 29th year.

With good fortune, wild birds, including those coming to your feeders, also can run up impressive numbers. Records from the Bird Banding Laboratory, operated by the U.S. Fish and Wildlife Service, show these longevity records for some of our common backyard species: Blue Jay, 17 years; Hairy Woodpecker, 15 years, American Crow, 14 years; American Robin, almost 14 years; House Sparrow, 13 years; Black-capped Chickadee, 12 years; American Goldfinch, 10 years.

The average life span of most adult songbirds is probably from two to five years. If birds survive to fledgling stage and into their first migration, prospects for life improve dramatically.

How do you tell how old a bird is? Most determinations separate immature birds from adults without providing an answer in calendar terms. An examination of the skull of a bird will offer clues to its maturity; bird banders use this method to separate juveniles from adults, gently blowing aside head feathers to see if skull sections have grown together. Many birds go through progressive molts, each new set of feathers announcing an age plateau. Most songbirds, however, achieve adult plumage within a year and succeeding molts offer no clues to advancing age.

Certain birds take longer to achieve full adult plumage, such as gulls and eagles. Bald Eagles take four to five years to show the full white head and tail of the adult. The intermediate plumages allow a knowledgeable person to tell that bird's age. Once adult plumage is achieved, the eagle is like some humans of a certain age—you're not sure and they won't tell.

— *Jim Williams*

Questions and Answers

bird behavior

Are they still discovering new species? My dad says no.

New birds are being discovered on a rather regular basis, on average two species per year, but they are not birds you are going to see in your backyard. For example, a new species of antpitta was discovered in Ecuador in 1998. A year earlier, scientists found a bird in Madagascar later named the Red-shouldered Vanga and a new woodcreeper was identified along the Amazon River. A species of warbler not seen since 1924 recently was rediscovered in the Cape Verde Islands.

Why do we rarely (never) see the bodies of birds that die?

Scavengers are the biggest reason. Most dead animals are eaten by something soon after they die. In your neighborhood, cats, skunks and perhaps raccoons take dead birds. Some predators will learn to routinely check beneath windows with which birds frequently collide. Another reason you don't often see dead creatures is that they die in hiding or under cover where they are not visible.

The birds in our yard sometimes seem to chase each other for no apparent reason. Do birds play?

While at least one noted ornithologist, Alexander Skutch of Costa Rica, believes that birds do play, it is hard to know why an individual bird is doing a particular thing. In the spring, birds are likely chasing each other as they define and defend their breeding territories. The next time you are Up North, however, pay attention to flying ravens and see if you can detect action that has any function other than play.

How high can birds fly?

The norm seems to be below 500'. During migration, species often are seen flying as high as 10,000'. Birds that migrate very long distances (thousands of miles) can sometimes be found at twice that height. There is a record of a flock of swans being seen at 29,000'.

I've observed the various types of birds taking turns coming to the feeders in the morning. First the chickadees, then House Finches and finally the House Sparrows (thank goodness they wait 'til last). Do these yard birds truly have some sort of pecking order or do some just become active earlier in the day?

There are two things at work here. Different species have different feeding habits. You will see more Northern Cardinals, for example, at dawn and dusk than at mid-day. And, yes, some species and some individuals are more assertive than others. Smaller birds usually will feed more often, larger birds less often but for longer periods of time. What you see at your birdfeeder might be viewed as a microcosm of the natural system which assigns each species a place.

We've seen birds in our garden squirming around in a patch of soft dry soil. What are they doing?

The birds are taking a bath, a dust bath, sometimes called dusting. Several species of birds do this, wriggling in sand or fine dry soil to fill their feathers with it, then shaking themselves clean. The birds often follow this with preening. Sparrows and wrens are birds you might see engaging in this practice. Why they do it is far from clear. It has been suggested that dusting removes excess moisture and preen oil from feathers, thus helping keep feathers fluffy, and that it might also flush out ectoparasites such as bird lice.

Do birds have a sense of smell?

Birds are equipped with the sensory apparatus for perceiving odors, but it is believed they use this sense far less than do mammals. Evidence of this seems to be scarce and sometimes conflicting. Some seabirds, albatrosses, shearwaters and storm-petrels, for example, apparently can detect odors at significant distances. And some experts believe that Turkey Vultures find some of their food by the smell of decaying flesh; this is disputed. The birds in your backyard most likely rely on visual clues to find food.

Questions and Answers

Q: Because birds have eyes on each side of the head, do they see two images, one from each eye? If so, how do they know which side is which?

A: Birds join the images captured by each eye to create a single perceived image, just as we do. Birds can also see from only one eye, as can we; they lose some depth perception when using only one eye.

Q: Where do birds go when it storms? Can birds anticipate bad weather?

A: Some birds take refuge in bird houses, tree cavities or other holes where protection is available. Other birds move to protected areas out of the wind, taking shelter in heavy bushes or dense evergreens. And some just tough it out. Heavy hail storms will kill birds, tornadoes are as dangerous to birds as to other creatures and strong winds or sudden changes in temperature can cause problems for migrating birds. We don't know if birds can anticipate bad weather.

Q: How many sets of eggs does a pigeon lay during one summer?

A: Four to five sets are typical, sometimes more. Pigeons in colder areas probably have fewer clutches. Pigeon, by the way, is a common term for Rock Dove.

Q: I've seen several partial albino birds in my back yard. I've seen a Common Grackle with white tail feathers, a partial albino House Finch and now I'm getting visits from a goldfinch which is white where it should be yellow. Is this common among birds?

A: It is more common in some species than in others. In all the mentioned species it is uncommon. And looking different, these birds stand out; you notice them more often.

Q: How long do little birds like goldfinches live?

A: A small bird like an American Goldfinch or Black-capped Chickadee might live eight or ten years or longer under ideal conditions. Even your backyard does not provide that ideal, however, so typical life expectancy for these smaller birds could be six months to a year or two.

Every now and then I see gulls flying over shopping centers. Why are these birds there?

Gulls are scavengers. They frequent places where they can find something to eat. Shopping centers are high on their list, along with parking lots and landfills. There are colonies of Ring-billed Gulls that nest on the flat pebble-covered rooftops of warehouses and other large buildings. To the birds, the roofs are like a beach. Another contributing factor might be that you are seeing gulls as they fly between their daytime hangouts and their nighttime roosting areas. The gulls will seek the safety of open water for sleep. One more thing: they aren't seagulls. These birds might never see salt water in their lifetimes. The species commonly seen here are Herring Gulls and Ring-billed Gulls. Bonaparte's Gulls and Franklin's Gulls move through the area during migration.

Why do some birds sing at night? I hear robins and other birds I can't identify singing well before the sun comes up.

Birds are not on the same schedule as humans, so singing at night or in the pre-dawn hours is normal as they go about their activities. Some birds sing only at night (Whip-poor-wills) or night and day (Sedge Wrens, Gray Catbird, Rose-breasted Grosbeak).

Why do the birds in our neighborhood stop singing about mid-summer?

In May and June, male birds sing to attract mates and to warn other males from their space. When incubation begins, he sings to let his mate know he is there. When the task turns to raising young, the male has less reason to sing and call attention to himself.

Do only male songbirds sing?

This is true for most species, but some females do sing and this is thought to be part of the species' courtship. Examples are the Baltimore Oriole, House Finch, Gray Catbird and Northern Cardinal. Some species, such as the Barred Owl, Carolina Wren and Gray-cheeked Thrush, sing duets during which males and females call to each other for periods of time. Note that most species have contact calls that both birds use to stay in touch, so to speak.

According to my bird identification book, American Goldfinches are not migratory. But ours are gone now. Why?

American Goldfinches are migratory, but only for short distances, not enough distance to influence range maps in your book. Consider them nomadic. The birds you had moved on, probably to the south. You might still see more goldfinches this winter, most likely birds visiting from the north.

Every year great numbers of birds come through my yard during spring migration, except this year. Why are some spring migrations different?

Finches sometimes don't go south for the winter, so you wouldn't see those birds returning north in the spring. And migrants coming from the south have to wait for acceptable weather and food conditions. If spring is slow, what we can get is a strong but short push of migrants in late May and early June. If you blinked, you would have missed it. Abundance of birds and the timing of their migration varies from year to year.

We have juncos at our feeders in winter. They are not here in the summer. Where do they go then?

Dark-eyed Juncos nest from Lake Superior far into Canada, coast to coast, and into Alaska. They winter from the southern portions of western Canada throughout the lower 48 United States.

We read about winter birds visiting here from far away, like the Varied Thrush. What happens to those wanderers when spring comes?

Most of these visitors got lost; that's why they were here. Some of them move on, returning to their usual habitat. Others die, victims of predators or weather or the physiological malfunction that caused them to go astray. A Varied Thrush seen in Duluth for ten weeks one recent winter eventually was found frozen in a yard where it had been visiting feeders.

When do the robins return in the spring?

Though the area in general hosts small numbers of American Robins every winter, the bulk of them spend the cold months south of here, where food is easier to find. They begin to return in noticeable numbers in March.

This spring and summer we had three robin nests in our yard with two to four babies in each nest. Our yard should be full of robins now, but we don't see any. Where do they go in late summer?

When the young birds leave the nest, but before they can fly, they stay hidden because of their vulnerability to predators. Even so, neighborhood cats could have killed many of these youngsters. As soon as they can fly, the birds disperse to find food; other habitat might have offered better feeding opportunities.

We see robins in our yard after the ground freezes in the fall and before it thaws in the spring. How can they find worms to eat if the ground is frozen?

The early and late birds catch more than worms. Robins eat berries, fruit (keep an eye on apple trees, particularly crab apples, once the weather turns cold), nuts, meal worms, snails, insects, even bread or popcorn. This varied diet allows them to survive when earthworms are in the deep freeze. Small numbers of robins spend the winter where there is snow and ice almost every year. Look for them around open water where there are fruit or berry trees.

Why do we always see flocks of starlings? Other birds seem to come in ones or twos.

Many birds flock in the fall and spring. Geese, swans, crows, cranes, blackbirds and other species gather in these seasons to roost or migrate. Some birds are communal by nature, moving through the year in flocks. European Starlings and Cedar Waxwings, for example, are usually found in groups.

We see pigeons only in the city. Where did pigeons live before the city was here?

The bird commonly called pigeon is officially known as the Rock Dove. Rock Doves nest in nonurban settings on rocky cliffs and also in rural areas; they love barns and silos, feeding on spilled grain when not wheeling over the farmstead. They are native to Europe.

What do Canada Geese eat?

Canada Geese love fresh green grass, which helps explain their proliferation in our yards and parks. They also eat roots, seeds, grains and insects.

How many times a season will a Canada Goose nest?

Only once, assuming the first attempt is successful; if the nest or eggs are destroyed, the pair often will try again. Canada Geese take longer to mature than some smaller birds, which leaves no opportunity for the parents to raise a second family. You will notice family groups from hatching until fall migration.

The Mississippi River near my home stays open all winter, but I don't see any ducks there. Why not? Are there places along the river where ducks and geese stay during the winter? Do swans ever over-winter here?

There are ducks on the river in the winter, but they prefer to stay in places where there is lots of room, good cover and food and not much movement to the water. Generally, swans don't stay in this area for the winter, although you will find a large flock of Trumpeter Swans on the Mississippi River near the Monticello, Minnesota nuclear power plant. Ducks can often be found on open lakes and ponds throughout the area. If you can find a body of water kept open by discharge of warm water, that is a good place to look for wintering waterfowl.

Are the ducks we see on and around city lakes tame or wild?

Generally, these ducks and others can be considered wild, though they have lost much of their natural fear of humans. Mallard is the species most likely to be seen.

We saw Tundra Swans on an area lake this spring, resting in a bay near our home. Are swans edible? Are they hunted?

Swans are edible. They are vegetarians and are said to roast up nicely. However, it is against the law to take swans; Tundra and Trumpeter Swan species are protected here. Your swan dinner would cost you much more than you imagine.

Hunters and fishermen say that game species are more active at certain times of the day, depending on sun and moon cycles. Do birds respond to the same stimulus?

Yes, generally speaking. Watch the activity at your backyard feeder through the day for a series of days and see if you can detect a shift in the time of heavy feeding activity.

Why are Killdeer protected by federal law?

All migratory nongame birds are protected. Prior to enactment of federal legislation establishing such protection, certain species were reduced to the brink of extinction by market hunting and so-called sport shooting. Species deemed suitable for the pot and frying pan can legally be taken during established seasons. Limits are set to control the harvest and retain a viable population level.

Every time I walk in the empty lot next door to us a Killdeer comes from nowhere and seems to get upset. I can't figure out how I am bothering this bird. Can you offer any insight?

It is likely that the bird has a nest nearby. Killdeer nest on the ground, often on open stretches of gravel or rocks. They have been known to nest in the middle of driveways or parking lots. They do not need to be near water. Watch the bird for its distraction display. It will feign injury in an attempt to lure you from its nest.

Why do nuthatches climb down trees instead of up?

Nuthatches eat insects and insect eggs when they can find them and even chase and catch flying insects on occasion. They also eat seeds from a variety of wild plants. They will also come to your feeders year-round for suet and seeds. It is believed that nuthatches climb downward because they can see food that was missed by birds that only climb upward. Did you ever lose your keys and find them by turning around so you could see spots you missed when you entered the room? That's the nuthatch trick.

Of the 24 species of nuthatches worldwide, two can be found in the central U.S.. The White-breasted Nuthatch is more common and a frequent visitor to yards and feeders.

Less widespread is the Red-breasted Nuthatch, which can be more easily found in northern regions. It prefers a habitat with spruce and fir trees. It is a migrant species that is highly irruptive (moving sporadically in large numbers) and, probably because of this, is the only nuthatch to have actually crossed the Atlantic Ocean! It migrates northward to its breeding grounds from early April through late May. Look for it in the area at that time. (Birders of good fortune might have one spending the winter in their neighborhood.)

The Red-breasted Nuthatch has the peculiar habit of smearing the opening of its nest hole with sticky tree resin. This is probably to deter predators. Its white-breasted cousin uses the bodies of noxious insects for the same purpose. Nuthatches avoid the goo by flying directly into the hole rather than flying to the tree and climbing in. This is unusual (and it requires good brakes).

The name nuthatch comes from the way the bird eats by wedging a nut into the bark of a tree then "hacking" it open with its bill. Nut-hack became nuthatch.

Why are the most common birds of winter in this region—the chick-adees, nuthatches and Downy and Hairy Woodpeckers—all black and white or shades of gray?

This is a subject for a thesis. Briefly, it is assumed coloration provides camouflage for the bird. The dark top and light bottom color patterns of these birds help them blend into their environment when seen from any angle. Dark colors also more readily absorb heat from the sun. The white flashes in wing or tail that you see when the bird takes flight are thought by some to startle pursuers, giving the fleeing bird a momentary advantage. Of course, not all birds commonly seen in the winter lack bright color. Consider the Northern Cardinal, Blue Jays, both crossbills, Common Redpolls, Pine and Evening Grosbeaks and House and Purple Finches.

What would chickadees eat during the winter if we didn't feed them?

There is a surprising amount of natural food available for these and other birds wintering here. After all, they've been doing it quite successfully for a long, long time. Chickadees eat seeds, insect eggs and berries, among other things. Experts estimate that birds which come to feeders take 20 percent of their needed nourishment from the feeder, finding the other 80 percent from natural sources.

Do Blue Jays eat small birds like chickadees during the winter?

No. Blue Jays are known to take very young birds from nests. They don't attack and eat adult birds.

Do all states in the Upper Midwest see the same birds each year?

Yes and no. Adjacent states are most likely to share the same bird species. But birds are habitat specific and when habitat changes, particularly as it does when you go west or south, species change as well. The farther you travel from home, the greater the likelihood of more birds being different from those you usually see.

How many species are native to Minnesota, Wisconsin and Michigan?

Native is a relative term, subject to discussion. If native means nesting, about 250 species have nested in the three states during the past quarter century. A handful of these are uncommon, however, not nesting here every year. Other species once nested here but now do so rarely if ever (Burrowing Owl and Barn Owl are two examples). The infamous House Finch is a very recent addition to our nesting list and the Eurasian Collared-Dove is beginning to be seen in small numbers; its population is sure to grow. Five species that nest here (Rock Dove, Ring-necked Pheasant, Gray Partridge, European Starling and House Sparrow) are imports, not native in the true sense of the word. If native means seen here every year (but not necessarily nesting), the list grows from 250 to more than 300 species. And if native means any species ever found here, the list moves to more than 400 species (not including the imports). For our money, we would suggest that nesting birds—250 species—are native, just as you are native if born and raised here.

books about birds

I am using a bird book that was printed in 1969. Is there any reason for me to buy a new one? Are new ones better in some way?

You will find some bird name changes in newer books, along with better illustrations in some cases and new information, things learned about this and that in the past 30+ years. Most likely to change will be the maps showing where species are found. The very recent movement of House Finches into the central portion of the United States is a good example of bird populations in flux. Go ahead and treat yourself to a new book.

Is there an inexpensive book that would help me identify and learn about the birds that come to my feeder?

The Minnesota Department of Natural Resources has published a book entitled *Wild About Birds* by Carrol Henderson. This is the best book you can buy for backyard birdfeeding. It contains excellent color photographs of feeder birds, plus tips on feeding and attracting birds.

Is there any site on the Internet that will give me information about the birds that come to my yard and my feeders?

There are many such sites, many of which are linked to more sites yet. It goes on and on. The Minnesota Ornithologists' Union website has links to other sites which might be a beginning point for you. The MOU site is at www.cbs.umn.edu/~mou.

Try Wild Birds Forever at www.birdsforever.com or The Backyard Birding Page at www.bcpl.net/~tross/by/backyard.html. Another site is Peterson Online at www.petersononline.com/. Wild Bird magazine contains regular features about interesting bird websites and other bird magazines might offer similar information.

Are video tapes a good way to learn to identify birds? If so, can you recommend specific tapes?

Video tapes can be an excellent way to become familiar with birds and more skilled in their identification. If you do this, watch the tapes more than once. Listen closely to songs, for all tapes will give you bird sounds as well as visuals. If you have a field guide that you use for bird identification, consult it during the video to help match the living, moving bird with the static drawing in the book. Which videos are best? There are many. Start with tapes which contain the names of authors or publishers you recognize. Ask for a brief demonstration before you buy. Make sure that the birds presented are birds of your area.

My parents, who are partially deaf, would love to hear bird songs. Are there tape recordings of bird songs?

Yes. You can find such tapes and CDs in birding specialty stores or in other shops selling birding equipment or natural history items. Some popular sets are keyed to bird identification guides. You often find them in sets for either the eastern or western parts of the U.S. For this area, buy the eastern version.

birds throughout the year

Spring Migrants in **Your Backyard**

First bird to indicate spring? That's the robin, right?

Nope.

By the time migrant American Robins reach your yard, Horned Larks, the real sign of winter on the wane, have been pecking at rural roadsides for several weeks. Larks are little fellows you might see on road shoulders or in fields blown clean of snow. When disturbed, they run first, then fly off in a wide circle, to settle down behind you or farther down the road, where you can set them to flight again.

They begin to arrive here as early as mid-January, even though that sounds incredibly optimistic. Most of the larks which will nest here have arrived by the end of March. A few tough larks even winter here.

Your backyard also has early bird visitors that might well be seen before the traditional robin.

Male Red-winged Blackbirds generally are in marshy areas in southern Minnesota, Wisconsin and Michigan by early March. The males arrive before the females to establish nesting territories. They travel in flocks large and small, and their communal conversations in the morning and evening as they leave or return to roosting sites are easy to notice. Blackbirds will come to your feeders or to food scattered on the ground. They love black oil sunflower seeds.

Kinglets are other birds which can be seen as early as March. There are two kinds of kinglets here, the Ruby-crowned and the Golden-crowned. You can see the bright yellow top-of-the-head mark on the latter, but don't expect to see the ruby on the former; it is for special display only. Both birds have interesting coloration of bright bonnets over rather plain jackets; look for a pair of lighter bars on their wings. The Golden-crowned Kinglet arrives first.

Kinglets are small birds, fully 1" smaller than a Black-capped Chickadee. You might recognize them best by their actions. They don't lack for action, particularly the Ruby-crowned Kinglet. This bird is constantly in motion, examining tree branches for insects, flitting from branch to branch, hardly ever giving you a good look. A small hyperactive bird in early spring is probably a kinglet.

Kinglets nest along the Canadian border and north. Most of them will be on nesting grounds in early May.

There are several species of sparrows that you can see in your yard or neighborhood. Fox Sparrows, large for sparrows and reddish, return in March. Listen for them scratching in leaf litter under bushes. Song Sparrows are here then, too. They are best identified by the stick-pin spot in the center of their well-striped breast. The stripes are important marks because American Tree Sparrows, which winter here, also have a center-breast spot, but on a clear breast. White-throated Sparrows make another early arrival. They have sharply defined white throats, black and white stripes atop their heads and plain gray breasts. (Pull out your field guide and take a look at the sparrows. They're not plain little brown birds that all look alike. Really.)

White-throats are easily known by their song. Once you recognize it, you can bird from your bed if you sleep near an open window. The White-throat will be singing at dawn. Translated to English, the bird sings, "Poor *old* Pea-bo-dy Pea-bo-dy Pea-bo-dy," the second note clearly falling and the rhythm unmistakable.

Swamp Sparrows are here with the others, as are Lincoln's Sparrow and White-crowned Sparrows. That makes seven sparrow species in the spring before we're safely out of snow danger. Sparrows are birds of the brush and ground. Build a brush pile, maybe 2' high and 4' in diameter and you will please sparrows. Feed them by scattering sunflower seeds on the brush pile and the dirt surrounding it.

You might create a temporary sparrow spot in a corner of your garden or a flower bed. By the time you want to plant, the sparrows will be gone to their nesting sites.

For many of us, warblers are the highlight of the spring migration.

More than thirty species of warblers either nest in Minnesota, Wisconsin and Michigan or pass through on their way to Canada. Each is a small (about 5") slender bird. Most are brightly and distinctly marked with three or four colors straight from the crayon box. Most warblers during migration will be seen in trees, often in upper branches.

The first warbler to look for is the Yellow-rumped Warbler, aptly named. It is an early arrival. Start checking the trees in your yard in late March and early April. Look for a bird with yellow on its lower back, just above the tail. The male of this species will be more definitively marked with black and white on its face. Another early warbler is the Palm Warbler. Watch for a warm brown bird with yellowish underparts that bobs its tail. That tail movement is your best clue.

Warblers often move in small flocks called waves. Several species might flock together and be joined by chickadees and nuthatches as they forage. Finding a wave of warblers in your trees on a bright spring morning is a very good way to start your day. — *Jim Williams*

Birds in the Fall

The birds of spring arrive with a bang, like Gene Kelly on the movie screen, arms swinging, feet tapping, song filling the theater. "Here I AM!"

It's different in the fall.

You might have noticed that bird-wise your neighborhood is quieter in the fall. The decibel drop began in July, when male birds of nesting pairs essentially stopped territorial singing, song being the main defense of home turf. Even early morning bird song, romantically seen as joyous welcome of the new day, diminished.

I could lie in bed as day lightened in June and easily count 10 or 12 different birds by song alone. Now I hear chickadees, nuthatches, Blue Jays and crows. Most other birds have gone silent or gone south.

Well, we still have Common Grackles and blackbirds with us, both raucous at times, particularly the young birds, begging for food at a time when they should be self-sufficient, at least working on a part-time basis.

The migrants that blew through here last May have been drifting back for the past 60 days or so. You might have missed the warblers, vireos and thrushes we expect to enjoy in May. We sometimes have unusual migrations. It's a complicated subject, but one reason is fine, even weather with no cold or wet fronts to stop migration and bring birds to ground where we all can see them. Some experts say spring birds simply fly over us sometimes.

You might still find some of these migrants in your yard. The males will be in basic plumage and probably not singing. Basic plumage means the birds molted out of bright breeding plumage (described in official terms as alternate plumage even though it is the look known best and considered by many birdwatchers as essential to identification). For the most part, the birds work their way to wintering grounds in plain duds, the need to impress a mate shelved until next spring.

Watch for small bands of birds, mixed flocks of warblers, vireos, kinglets and gnatcatchers. Listen for chickadees and nuthatches, often found with the migrants and more apt to be vocal. Just wander the tree line, watching and listening. Parks and cemeteries are good places to go right now, or the paths around local lakes. Look up and check out those chickadees.

If you intend to feed this winter, there are some birdfeeder chores for you. Now is as good a time as any to get them done.

Take down your feeders and clean them. Shake out the hulls, scrape off the moldy collection of sodden seeds on the tray. Washing in a mild bleach/water solution is a good idea. Dry the feeders thoroughly before refilling them and putting them back into action.

You might want to take a broom rake and scatter the hulls which have fallen into your grass. Some folks rake them to piles and carry them away. I am of the nature's helper school, believing that the seed shells are tiny bits of yard food, full of important nutrients, to be left right where they are. (There are two opinions on this subject, each side often represented by persons married to each other.)

Don't take down your hummingbird feeder just yet, for late hummers are still on the move, perhaps even a stray of a species not often seen here. Examine all fall hummingbirds closely; you never know who might visit. Do clean your hummingbird feeder, though, and keep it freshly filled.

Don't worry: you will not entice the hummingbirds to stay in your yard beyond their usual departure date, condemning them to frostbite. The birds know where they should go and when they should leave. That applies to seed-eaters as well. You can help fuel their departure; it is highly unlikely you will prevent it.

Visit your neighborhood bird supply store. Treat yourself to a new feeder. If your present feeder hangs, buy one for a post or vice versa. With two or more feeders, you can offer different varieties of seeds and perhaps attract additional species when sharp-edged weather arrives and serious birdfeeding begins.

Take a look at a new bird guide, too. You can always use another bird book to give you more information about bird identification and there are many new guide books from which to choose. — *Jim Williams*

Birds in the Winter

One recent winter, in the morning when I went to the end of the driveway to find my morning paper, I often put to wing a pair of Mourning Doves which had spent the night roosting above our front door. They somehow found space on the trim there, tucking themselves in beneath the wide soffit, facing south, out of the worst of the wind.

I should have gone out the back door at least once, to peek around the corner of the house and see if they slept one against the other. I'll bet they did.

A warm place to sleep, even warmer by a few degrees in a leeward roost, is critical to birds in winter. Finding such a place is one of several challenges they face here. And sleeping side to side would be even better, two warm bodies sharing precious calories. Many birds do sleep that way.

Shelter and food and water—there you have a bird's short list of survival necessities. If you bring birds to your yard, you can help them with all three during our winter months.

Shelter is something you can provide for certain birds. The species which nest in cavities, and these include some of the most popular brands—chickadees, nuthatches and woodpeckers—will, on occasion, use a dormitory designed to help keep them warm during cold weather. This roosting box is similar to a bird house but with the entry hole low on the front panel to help hold body heat as it rises in the box. One design calls for a box 12" square and 3' deep. Inside, grooves are cut on one wall to aid woodpeckers in roosting, with small dowels protruding from another inside wall as perches for birds.

Mount the box on a pole with a predator guard beneath it. Place the box in a sheltered spot, out of prevailing winds. A box which faces south to catch some sun will be warmer.

Food is the most obvious kind of assistance for winter birds. We put out feeders and supply seeds and suet. This is helpful, but it might surprise you to know that it isn't critical. Except in the worst of weather, the birds that visit your feeders find about 80 percent of their food elsewhere, from natural sources.

If you take a long weekend for skiing or snowmobiling and return to find your feeders empty, don't fret about the birds. They didn't starve. The biggest problem might be your own enjoyment. If the feeders are empty too long, the birds will re-route themselves to other food sources, taking your yard off the list. Birds have wonderful memories when it comes to finding food. They remember where it is. And where it isn't. Keep your feeders full if you want the continuing company of yard birds.

It's also a good idea to clean the feeders a couple of times a year. Feeders are like windows; fall is a good time to put the shine on them.

Generally speaking, you can increase the number of birds coming to your feeders by putting up more feeders. If you have one, try two or three. If you have three, upgrade to five or six. Don't put all the feeders in one place. Offer a variety of seeds. Designating a patch of lawn or garden for birds that prefer to feed on the ground (doves, sparrows, juncos) also will help attract more birds. Creating a small brush pile near your seed scatter is helpful. Birds like the security the brush shelter offers.

You could take your hummingbird feeders down now. Take them apart and wash them thoroughly before you put them away. Or you could leave the feeders in place until temperatures drop below freezing. Occasionally, hummers show up late in the fall. Often, these birds are of species other than our usual Ruby-throated Hummingbird, rare visitors, usually from western states.

A tip about storing birdseed: don't keep it in the house. Seed can harbor a terrible nuisance called the India meal moth. This is not the fault of your birdseed vendor. It simply is birdseed reality. Given a warm place to live, these moths will breed and lay eggs. The eggs will hatch larvae. The larvae will become moths. And so on, forever. I know from personal experience you will wear yourself out trying to get rid of them. Keep the seed outside or in the garage, preferably in a covered metal container.

I have been told that a couple of days outside in freezing temperatures will kill the moths or larvae, making the seed safe for your pantry or basement shelf. But having been there and done that, I keep my seed in the garage. Period.

Birds need water in winter. The season makes no difference, except winter makes water more difficult to find. A heated birdbath can be a most welcome attraction for birds in your neighborhood. You can purchase simple heating elements which you place in the water in the birdbath. New are birdbaths with such elements built in. In either case, you need a grounded outdoor electric outlet and a grounded extension cord. Check the birdbath often, for dry winter days cause rapid evaporation. — *Jim Williams*

About Backyard Birds

The answers to questions and the essays in this book are based to a large degree on the personal experiences of the authors. Much assistance, however, came from the work of other writers. These publications were used on a routine basis as our information was assembled and checked, and we are indebted to these fellow birders. Any errors found in this book, however, belong solely to its authors.

Bibliography

Atlas of Breeding Birds of Michigan. Richard Brewer, Gail A. McPeek, and Raymond J. Adams Jr. Michigan State University Press. East Lansing, Michigan. 1991.

Birds in Minnesota. Robert B. Janssen. University of Minnesota Press, Minneapolis, Minnesota. 1987.

Birdwatcher's Companion, The. Christopher Leahy. Portland House, New York, New York. 1982.

Bluebird Trails: A Guide to Success, 3rd ed. Edited by Dorene Scriven. The Bluebird Recovery Program of the Audubon Chapter of Minneapolis, Minneapolis, Minnesota. 1999.

Checklist of the Birds of Minnesota. Minnesota Ornithological Records Committee. Minnesota Ornithologists' Union, Minneapolis, Minnesota. 1999.

Dictionary of American Bird Names, The, rev. edition. Ernest A. Choate. The Harvard Common Press, Boston, Massachusetts. 1985.

Guide to the Nests, Eggs, and Nestlings of North American Birds. A. Paul J. Baicich and Colin J. O. Harrison. Academic Press, New York, New York. 1997.

Field Guide to the Birds of Eastern and Central North America, 4th ed. Roger Tory Peterson. Houghton Mifflin, New York, New York. 1980.

Field Guide to the Birds of North America, National Geographic Society, 3rd ed. National Geographic Society, Washington, D.C. 1999.

Landscaping for Wildlife. Carrol Henderson, Carolyn J. Dindorf, Fred J. Rozumalski. Minnesota Department of Natural Resources, St. Paul, Minnesota. 1998.

Lives of North American Birds. Kenn Kaufman. Houghton Mifflin, New York, New York. 1996.

Minnesota Birds: Status and Occurrence. Anthony X. Hertzel, Robert B. Janssen, Peder H. Svingen. Peder H. Svingen, Minneapolis, Minnesota. 2000.

Wild About Birds: The DNR Bird Feeding Guide. Carrol Henderson. Minnesota Department of Natural Resources, St. Paul, Minnesota. 1995.

Wisconsin Birdlife: Population and Distribution. Samuel D. Robbins, Jr. University of Wisconsin Press, Madison, Wisconsin. 1991.

Woodworking for Wildlife: Homes for Birds and Mammals. Carrol Henderson. Minnesota Department of Natural Resources, St. Paul, Minnesota. 1992.

Questions and Answers

index

Questions and Answers

sugar water, 68
thistle seed, 8, 11, 12, 42
year-round feeding, 12, 13
Fruit, 15, 16
birds that eat fruit, 12, 16, 68, 73, 85-87, 103, 113
dried fruit, 8, 12, 16, 18
fruit-bearing trees, 10

G

Garden beds, 56
Geese, 113, 114
Gnatcatcher, Blue-gray 102, 125
Goldeneye, Common, 98
Goldfinch, American, 99, 107, 110, 112
attracting, 11
foods eaten, 7-9, 15, 99
Goose, Canada, 113, 114
Grackle, Common, 53, 102, 106, 110, 124
control methods, 8, 53
foods eaten, 7, 8, 14
Grains, 14, 73, 114
Grapes, 12
Grebe, Pied-billed, 101
Grit, 16
Grosbeak, Black-headed, 100
Evening, 7, 16, 116
Pine, 116
Rose-breasted, 12, 100, 111
Ground-feeding, 15, 19, 86, 89
recommended foods, 7, 8, 55
when/where to ground-feed, 10, 11, 15
Ground-nesting, 31, 102, 115
Grouse, 104
Gull, 76, 77, 107, 111
Bonaparte's, 77
discouraging, 51
Franklin's, 77
Herring, 77, 111
Ring-billed, 77, 111

H

Hackberry, 10
Hawk, 52, 98
hawk calls to discourage crows, 45
Sharp-shinned, 52
Hawthorn, 10
Hearts and parts, see: Foods and Feeding
Heart trouble in birds, 13
Herbicides, 14
Heron, 97
Highbush Cranberry, 10
Honeysuckle, 69, 73, 74

Houses, see Birdhouses
Hummingbird, 67-71, 125
Ruby-throated, 67-71
moth that resembles, 69

I

Ice on feeders, 12, 55
Identifying birds, 93-105
things to look for, 94, 95, 100
Injured birds,
bird faking injury, 115
helping injured bird, 59
Insect-eating birds, 8, 30, 73, 83, 85-87, 89, 100, 103, 113, 116, 117
Insect infestation in birdseed, 13, 14
eliminating, 54, 127
Intelligence of birds, 43, 44, 54
Internet sites about birds, 118
Invertebrates, 11, 80, 86, 113

J

Jay, 7, 16, 42
Blue, 16, 43, 107, 116, 124
foods eaten, 7-9, 15, 17, 18, 117
nesting, 27
Gray, 43
Jelly, 12, 68, 71
Junco, 97, 112
Dark-eyed, 7, 112
foods eaten, 7, 8
Gray-headed, 97
Oregon, 97
recommended feeder types, 15
Slate-colored, 97
Juneberry, 10
Juvenile birds, 13, 33, 86, 100, 103, 104, 107

K

Killdeer, 31, 34, 51, 102, 115
Kinglet, 103, 121, 125
Golden-crowned, 103, 121, 122, 125
Ruby-crowned, 103, 122, 125
Kitchen scraps, 15, 16, 18

L

Landscaping, 10
Lark, Horned, 121
Lifespan and longevity, 106, 107, 110
Loon, Common, 79

M

Magpie, Black-billed, 43
Mallard, 8, 15, 114
Mammals,
attracted to feeding stations, 17, 37-42

132

About Backyard Birds

Other books you'll enjoy from Adventure Publications

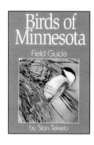  

Birds of Minnesota Field Guide; $12.95

Birds of Wisconsin Field Guide; $12.95

Birds of Michigan Field Guide; $12.95

Birds of Iowa Field Guide; $12.95

Wildflowers of Minnesota Field Guide; $16.95

Wildflowers of Wisconsin Field Guide; $16.95

Wildflowers of Michigan Field Guide; $16.95

Critters of Minnesota Pocket Guide; $5.95

Critters of Michigan Pocket Guide; $5.95

For more information call Adventure Publications at 1-800-678-7006 or mail us at P.O. Box 269, Cambridge, Minnesota, 55008